WAYMARKS

WAYMARKS

The Notre Dame Inaugural Lectures in Anthropology

KENNETH MOORE, EDITOR

UNIVERSITY OF NOTRE DAME PRESS
NOTRE DAME, INDIANA

"Body, Brain, and Culture" by
Victor Turner is reprinted by permission
from *Zygon* 18, no. 3 (1983): 221–245.

Library of Congress Cataloging-in-Publication Data

Waymarks: the Notre Dame inaugural lectures in anthropology

Bibliography: p.
Includes index.
1. Anthropology. I. Moore, Kenneth, 1930–
GN29.W38 1987 306 86-40339
ISBN 0-268-01939-8

Manufactured in the United States of America

To Victor Turner
Mentor, Colleague, and Exemplar

Contents

Acknowledgments

As we recall the early difficulties of organizing a department of anthropology at Notre Dame, we also recall those who supported our efforts and shared with us a knowledge of the possibilities a new department opened for the faculty, the University, and our successors. The process was initiated by Acting Dean Robert Burns in his recommendation to the Provost, Timothy O'Meara. We all agreed to proceed and see what developed. After a year of planning and presentations to university committees, Notre Dame President, Father Theodore Hesburgh, gave final approval based on the recommendations of the College and Academic councils.

The Notre Dame Inaugural Lectures commenced in our first year and were developed thoughtfully in consultation with Professors Leo Despres, James Bellis, Irwin Press, Carl O'Nell, Evelyn Early, Patrick Gaffney, and Ronald Berg. Continuing concern and support for the series was forthcoming from Michael Loux, currently Dean of the College of Arts and Letters. James Langford, Director of the Notre Dame Press has been personally involved with the series since its inception and the Department particularly appreciates his efforts and those of the Press staff in the production of this volume. Our gratitude is also extended to Dr. Richard Faber for his early reading of the text, and to Professors Fabio Dasilva, Bonnie Kettel and David Kettel for their comments on the final draft. Professors Martin Murphy and Hamilton Bims provided expertise in production. The cooperation of Carole Roos in the editing, mostly by overseas mail, was exemplary.

Finally, somewhere in this text it should be noted that the first anthropology course at Notre Dame was taught by the late Raymond W. Murray, C.S.C. We remember him not for this alone but for his daily contribution to the spirit of tolerance that is rightly associated with the teaching of anthropology at Notre Dame, as in so many other places. Each year an award is given in his name to the outstanding graduate in anthropology.

Introduction

The five distinguished lectures in this volume are summary statements by leading anthropologists which were originally presented at the University of Notre Dame to celebrate the joining of the scholarly traditions of anthropology with those of the University. As a series they provided members of the Notre Dame community a vital sense of this new discipline in their midst. Here they are shared with an interested readership as exemplary presentations of anthropological scholarship in the 1980s.

As we assemble this collection we are mindful that the readership will include those with a general interest in anthropology as well as professionals in the discipline. Both will find in the essays discussion at the highest level of current theoretical issues, unequivocating statements of position, and informed analyses in the anthropological mode. Reading these works, one is reminded of how and why anthropology cannot be understood as simply a modestly variant homologue of either a traditional social science or one of the disciplines of the humanities. The scope of its inquiry is grand and its paths to understanding are varied. History has given it a special role to play and an awareness of this is integral to the practice of the profession. A sense of scope and role are manifest in this collection by a particular concern with what unifies anthropology as against diversifying pressures peculiar to the discipline. That problems inherent in unity-diversity tensions could impede anthropology in fulfilling all the possibilities its distinctive role allows is a recurring and predominating theme, and more than any other defines the collection.

The problem of unity and diversity in anthropology has at least three dimensions, and in this volume the reader will encounter informed analysis of each. In one dimension there is the nature-culture issue in which the biological and psychic unity of mankind and the diverse enculturation processes of the world are seen to be of variable significance in explaining what humans do. In another dimension the search for universals and ultimately universal theories in the study of culture is seen as the proper focus of anthropology as against emphasis on explaining what is taking place within cultures. This is an issue of long standing in anthropology evoking such familiar names as Lewis Henry Morgan, Franz Boas, Robert Lowie, Leslie White, and Julian Steward. There is, finally, the problem of unity in the discipline, expressed in this collection as paradigmatic unity and all that it implies, as against the diversifying influences of specialized fields of study that have tended to proliferate in recent years.

The problem in its various aspects emerges in this work as part of fascinating discussions of specific topics, such as the importance of brain neurophysiology in the study of ritual or the development of types of violence in an evolutionary process, to name but two. Equally so, it is within five different perspectives that the reader encounters discussion of anthropology's role and strategies for fulfilling it. That this reflection on fundamentals takes place against a background of understanding from the history and philosophy of science enhances its value. Underlining the significance of this discussion, we elaborate that background here, providing the reader with an appropriate context for further reflection. We specifically utilize the insights of Thomas Kuhn and Michel Foucault, two historians of science who have had enormous influence on the ways that scholarly practitioners, including those in this volume, conceptualize what they do and what they are part of. Before proceeding, we will briefly summarize each of the papers to give a preliminary sense of the whole.

In the first lecture, Robin Fox utilizes evidence from the history of philosophy and the human sciences to present his case for an entirely new perspective and direction in anthropological research. He identifies anthropology as heir to "the humanist, empiricist liberal tradition that started with the Renaissance, coalesced in the Enlightenment, and became a serious political force in the nineteenth century." He identifies a "split mind" in anthropology in two conceptions of culture, one based in the materialist, reformist view of Tylor, and the other from the work of Matthew Arnold, emphasizing the integration of meaning. Fox criticizes contemporary anthropology for failing to keep faith with its evolutionary origins and for overemphasis on the concept culture, even though no general theory has developed from it. He concludes that with its foundation in evolutionary thought anthropology was in a unique position to integrate the social and the biological in the study of the human. Using, among others, Darwin, Bradley, Durkheim, and G. H. Mead, he presents a case for studying the mix of ecology and behavior and proposes the concept *ethosystem* for the "total feedback system involving general species propensities and ecological subsystems." The essay elaborates this conception and suggests that a *scienzia nuova,* a new social science, will in the long run emerge, probably directly out of natural science.

John Bennett's essay identifies problems arising from the changing social order on a world-wide scale and the need for developing methods for studying this transformation. Anthropology, he reminds us, came into being in Western culture and represented it in studying the great range of primitive cultures in the world. The theory and methods of anthropology are those appropriate to the study of discrete cultures and are inadequate to problems of understanding the contradictory tendencies of an emerging pan-cultural world order as it takes shape in the modern era. Bennett says, "We believe that anthropology *must* be prepared to work at macro levels, transcending its preoccupation with the micro and local—but at the same time, providing a unique synthesis of the micro and macro . . ." appropriate to the world order as it has emerged. All cultures, according to Bennett, "are now bi-cultures." "That is, whatever they may possess of their traditional, relatively isolated past, they now share some components of the international style and its media of communication and thought." Anthropology's further mission, Bennett concludes, is to relate the study of the material and the spiritual in the search for a new ordering principle, the foundation of a new civilization.

Victor Turner takes a life's experience as a leader in the anthropological study of ritual as a basis for exploring recent work in cerebral neurology to produce a "genuine dialogue between neurology and culturology in the study of ritual process." This is a totally new path for Turner. He describes his contribution to this collection as "one of the most difficult I have ever attempted," as it has required him to submit to question axioms hallowed by his generation of anthropologists. Turner refers to the influence of Robin Fox regarding the importance of understanding what human means, "in the first place" in the study of cultural phenomena such as ritual. Turner examines Paul D. MacLean's model of the triune brain, made up of the reptilian, old mammalian, and neo-mammalian structures, successively evolved, and research on hemisphere lateralization to explore coadaptation, ritual, play, and creative processes. In this essay, Turner lays the ground work for a new nature-culture synthesis in the study of ritual.

In the fourth lecture, "Cultural Materialism: Alarums and Excursions," Marvin Harris responds to the polemic surrounding his research strategy since it has become a focus of anthropological discussion. The essay stands as the most inclusive and succinct statement of cultural materialism (C.M.) so far. Harris clarifies C.M.'s scientific foundations and its relation to bio-psychological givens. He distinguishes it from idealist strategies in terms of materialist and idealist conceptions of the causal priority of infrastructure, structure, and superstructure. He examines the problem of "quitting early" in idealist and eclectic strategies using Robert Lowie's work to illustrate how premature conclusions can be disproved by further ethnographic evidence. Harris expresses his irritation at the misrepresentation of C.M. which suggests that it ignores symbolic and religious features, or regards them as epiphenomenal. Using examples from India's sacred cattle complex and the Iranian revolution, Harris elaborates the relation between religion and economy in processes of change. He concludes with a commentary on causality in history and its relationship to human consciousness and will.

The final essay, the last lecture in the series, given by Eric Wolf, explores war and peace in man's biological and cultural evolution. Wolf concludes that there is little evidence to support Robert Ardrey's notion of early man as a killer ape "thirsty for blood, hungry for meat, and defending his territory." Recognizing the importance of species specific dispositions, Wolf nevertheless emphasizes that "All human drives are subject to cultural transformations that put them at the service of quite different social, economic, political, and ideological arrangements. These arrangements dictate when and how we may fight, eat, sleep, and have sex." Using ethnographic resources, Wolf looks at arrangements where violence is limited to interpersonal conflict and the conditions under which societies move from interpersonal to collective violence. He examines collective violence as it relates to evolving patterns of resource control and kinship systems, and evaluates population pressures as a factor in military escalation. Considering more complex political entities, Wolf concludes that we inhabit a world of multi-tiered conflicts, and that seeing all world conflicts in terms of the superpowers alone severely misreads the situation. The greatest single threat to the modern world develops from the current arrangements of power and order that are subject to the extraordinary destabilizing influence of the international economy.

With a sense of the collection's scope, we proceed to look at general themes. Though each essay is a seasoned exploration of a topic of primary interest to each author at this point in his career, what the essays say together is equally fascinating. We have described them as waymarks, for together they provide a lucid sense of where anthropology stands late in the twentieth century, particularly on those issues that commanded our attention fifty years ago, and will require responses from within the discipline fifty years hence. For example the nature-culture dimension of the unity-diversity issue is covered in one way or another in every essay. The strongest statement as to the relative importance of intrinsic human dispositions and characteristics comes from Robin Fox who has stated so succinctly in the past that man has the kinds of societies he has because he is the kind of species he is. Fox recognizes that cultures are diverse and different, but sees each as a particular manifestation "of general processes." Ecological context and species processes of communication account for "an enormous variety" of societal behavior. Victor Turner's essay summarizes recent findings on the evolution and structure of the brain, posing questions as to how these have consequences in modes of thought, particularly those manifest in ritual. "It is interesting to me," he states, "that a dominant symbol—every ritual has several of them —should replicate in its structural and semantic makeup what are coming to be seen as key neurological features of the brain and the central nervous system." Marvin Harris's research strategy gives primacy to bio-psychological givens. Their significance in cultural materialism is in providing the basis for developing "currencies" for measuring inputs and outputs of socio-cultural systems, making it possible to measure optimizing behavior. He also points out that infrastructures, the causal center of socio-cultural systems is that component of social life which most directly mediates the satisfaction of biogram drives, needs, and functions.

These essays reflect what is increasingly characteristic of

contemporary anthropology—the general acceptance of the intrinsic importance of the biological in the explanation of human behavior; or said in another way, almost no one at this time thinks of the human species as a *tabula rasa* on which culture is written. Some behavioral disciplines are able to ignore biology completely or give it short shrift. Identifying particular human propensities as essentially primate or mammalian or studying human dispositions as emergent in evolution are almost irrelevant to their concerns. In this collection we note that Wolf and Bennett accord less importance to biological givens than the other three. Nevertheless, Wolf carefully examines the conclusions of evolutionists as to the basic propensities of early man, and Bennett recognizes the importance of biological studies along with archaeology in the integration of anthropology. If there is a single recommendation in all the essays, it is not so much that cultural anthropologists should be more involved in biological research, but rather that they should be ever responsive to the biological dimensions of man and be prepared to incorporate pertinent research in that area into their holistic studies of humankind.

The search for universal theories of a species that is culturally diverse, another aspect of unity-diversity tensions, is covered extensively in these essays. It is not always easy to separate it, however, from the even more emphatically stated concern, the problem of unity within anthropology in an era in which the propensity to specialize appears to threaten the integrity of the discipline. Both Bennett and Fox discuss this problem at length, with Fox amusingly ridiculing a contemporary phenomena, those departments who try to appoint every conceivable specialist from marxist, feminist, and primatological anthropologists to, in California, para-normal anthropologists.

It is most significant that the notion of disciplinary integrity is stated most often in these essays through use of Thomas Kuhn's concept of paradigm. Four of the five authors either use the term paradigm in the Kuhnian sense or specifically refer to *The Structure of Scientific Revolutions.* This is by no means extraordinary. Kuhn's assumptions as to what constitutes a science have had enormous influence on the natural and behavioral sciences, and this collection illustrates the degree to which they have influenced anthropology's view of itself. The call for paradigmatic unity can be seen as a call for unity generally for Kuhn does not spell out any single mode or principle of integration, not even a unifying theory. What Kuhn says most basically is that science takes place in communities which are unified by paradigms. In his own words: "A paradigm is what members of a scientific community share, and conversely, a scientific community consists of men who share a paradigm." Not merely a set of rules, and more than a theory, a paradigm is composed of "the entire constellation of values and techniques" in a given scientific community and "concrete puzzle solving solutions" which are employed as "models and examples."

What Kuhn means by paradigmatic unity is conveyed not only by what he says, but the manner in which he reached his conclusions. As Kuhn explains initially he was a graduate student in physics prior to taking his degree in the history of science. Socialization in the scientific community of physics together with his research into the history of science enabled him to portray what appeared to him to be taking place within scientific communities. In the course of his research he spent a year among social scientists and was impressed by the number of overt disagreements among them on basic assumptions in problems and methods. Comparing the two experiences, the author concluded that "the practice of astronomy, physics, chemistry and biology normally fails to evoke the controversies over fundamentals that today seem endemic among, say, sociologists and psychologists." "Attempting to discover the source of that difference led me to recognize the role in scientific research of what I've since called paradigms."

One of the principle consequences of Kuhn's influential

work has been to produce among social scientists a yearning for paradigms. In psychology, sociology, economics, and anthropology, sessions entitled "In search of a paradigm for . . .," "Paradigmatic Unity in . . ." predictably appear in the programs of professional meetings. The concern is authentic and is probably better understood by behavioral scientists, in all its implications, than by natural scientists. In social systems (and among intellectual groupings no less than any other) integration, coherence, or systems of order in shared values and common purpose underlie effectiveness and continuity. But the question naturally emerges: Must integration in the behavioral sciences always exist on the model of the natural sciences? The preponderant position among our contributors is strongly affirmative. Harris, Bennett, and Fox are unquestionably committed to a traditional scientific model for anthropology. Victor Turner and Eric Wolf, respectively influenced by linguistics and history, do not voice this concern quite so strongly.

Looking at the spectrum of positions current in anthropology, we find some who are emphatically *not* concerned with anthropology's status as a science. Among those voicing that position is Clifford Geertz—referred to by Fox as having been lauded for giving the death blow to the search for universals. Geertz's position on paradigmatic unity supported by a general theory couldn't be clearer; "calls for a general theory of just about anything sound increasingly hollow, and claims to have one megalomanic. Whether this is because it is too soon to hope for a unified science, or too late to believe in it is, I suppose, debatable. But it has never seemed further away, harder to imagine, or certainly less desirable than it is right now" (1983, 4). The relativistic position of anthropologists like Geertz has a long history in anthropology, as does the counter-position —a search for universals, for scientific laws in the study of human collectivities. The "split mind" of anthropology shows no sign of healing. The old-fashioned relativists do not disappear. They utilize Wittgenstein, Heidegger,

Gadamer, Ricoeur, Burke, and Barthes to update and fortify their position; while the natural science model is as strong as it has ever been. The question that follows is: Should we use the criteria Kuhn developed from the natural sciences to evaluate the social sciences, or should we recognize that the social sciences are basically and fundamentally different? In her classic, *Philosophy in a New Key,* Susan Langer seems to suggest the latter:

> The physical sciences found their stride without much hesitation. Psychology and sociology tried to catch up but with mathematical laws they were never really handy. Psychologists have avowed their empiricism, their experimental techniques and the importance of general deductions. They said their lack of general laws and calculable results is due to the fact that psychology is but young. When physics was as old as psychology is now, it was a definite systematic body of highly general facts, and the possibilities of its future progress were clearly visible. (1942, 25)

If the social sciences are fundamentally different from the natural sciences, how is the difference to be understood? The best answer in recent years comes from Michel Foucault who, like Kuhn, is a historian of science, but whose background is the behavioral rather than the natural sciences.

In Foucault's major work, *The Order of Things,* which in the last ten years has gained a worldwide prominence approximating the influence of Kuhn's classic in its first decade, he probes the origin of the human sciences in the changing *epistemes* of western culture. In contrast to Kuhn's concept of paradigms, which are essentially exemplary ways of doing science within disciplines in a particular period of history, the concept episteme refers to the most fundamental ways in which an age perceives reality and its consequences for ways of knowing. Both Kuhn and Foucault are, of course, speaking of a cognitive order.

Kuhn's cognitive order exists within the scientific community; Foucault speaks of the cognitive order of an entire civilization in an era. He identifies a number of successive epistemes but only two, the classical and the modern, are pertinent to his explanation of the emergence of the human or social sciences.

In the classical episteme, extending from 1650 to 1800, the study of humanity was limited to representations of man, but man as an object of study was missing. It was an age of taxonomies and measurement, and history saw the past as ordered in terms of ideals, a utopian past. Foucault's method for identifying epistemes, called an "archaeology of knowledge," involves a study of all levels of discourse—seemingly unimportant letters, records, diaries of scholars of little consequence as well as the more important figures and their records—to identify the historical *a priori*, the underlying rules of cultural order. As with the replacement of one paradigm by another in the work of Kuhn, Foucault's epistemes displace each other abruptly, and the rupture occurs apart from rational or logical developments.

The human sciences as we know them had their beginning around 1800 in the break between the classical and the modern episteme. Transformations in that break in the study of life, language, and labor laid the foundation for a totally new conception of the human, and the possibility of the human sciences as we know them today. Biology displaced a classic natural history, particularly in conceptualizing a relation between organism and environment. Philology replaced grammar, giving temporality as well as structure to language. Economics was transformed by incorporating a concern with production to a prior focus limited to exchange. None of these by itself led to a study of man but all contributed to its foundations. The principle feature of the modern episteme was the emergence of man in totality and being as an object of study. This reconceptualization, developed from transformed models, allowed for the emergence of human sciences.

The study of man in the modern episteme continues to be influenced by the natural sciences and philosophy, as well as by the transformed constituent models and the related transformation in conceptions of man as object of study. The habitat of intellect that results is geometrically portrayed by Foucault as a three-dimensional figure, a space enclosed on three sides, each side seen as a plane, and the surface of a trihedron. Located on one plane are (a) the mathematical and physical sciences for which order is a deductive and linear linking together of evident or verified propositions. Facing it, on a single plane, are the (b) constituent models of biology, philology, and economics—function and norm, signification and system, conflict and rule. On the third plane (c) there is the model of philosophical thought, what Foucault calls reflection on the same. Viewing this epistemological trihedron as now constructed, the human sciences are excluded; that is, they cannot be found in any of its dimensions. They are, however, included in the enclosed space between the surfaces, a precarious position because the study of humanity can be carried out by selecting any single model or using a combination of them. It is within this space that man is conceptualized as that which can be studied empirically. According to Foucault, man is for the human sciences "that living being who from within the life to which he entirely belongs and by which he traverses, constitutes representations by means of which he lives, and on the basis of which he possesses the strange capacity of being able to represent to himself precisely that life."

Succinctly stated, Foucault's culturally based explanation states that the possibility of the human sciences derives from the existence of prior models of knowing, which before the modern episteme had not been used in the empirical study of the human species. The presence of these models together with the reconceptualization of man as that which can be known from empirical study are the preconditions for the emergence of the human sciences.

Foucault's conception of the human sciences explains their relative lack of paradigmatic unity as a normal condition, to be understood as emergent in the course of their early history as part of the modern episteme. Foucault sees all human sciences as interlocking and useful in interpreting one another, "their frontiers become blurred . . . and composite disciplines multiply endlessly."

Of particular interest are Foucault's conclusions regarding the relation of ethnology (cultural anthropology) to other sciences. Though all the human sciences have developed with reference to the models described in the surfaces of the trihedron, anthropology's special place is a product of history which has placed it at the interface of western culture and all the cultures of the world. Studying cultures without histories, anthropology de-emphasized the chronological discourse characteristic of western history. It gave greater emphasis to synchronic correlations that reveal structural invariables beneath the surface. Situated between the West and other cultures in a condition of bi-culturalism, anthropology tends to avoid "the representations that men in any civilization give themselves of themselves." Foucault sees anthropology as a counter science not because it is less rational or objective than the other human sciences, but because given its regular contact with other ways of knowing and its pursuit of that which is below consciousness it is always calling into question that which is established. Foucault sees the future of anthropology not in the copying of other sciences, but in the study of the unconscious in the history of other cultures—of understanding in other cultures that which they cannot understand themselves.

Foucault's conception of anthropology allows for an enlarged discussion of what anthropologists do, and how it contrasts with other disciplines. In practice anthropologists do appeal to the logical empiricism and mathesis of the natural sciences, to the constituent models of function and norm, conflict and rule, signification and system, and then again to the tradition of philosophical reflection and the methods of history. The distinctive products of anthropologists result from the various combinations of these models, e.g., biology and history, philosophy and linguistics, etc. This produces the all too apparent diversity, the eclecticism and the proliferation of specialized studies that so concern contemporary anthropologists.

Of equal importance is Foucault's emphasis on the historical role of anthropology working at the margins between western culture and the traditional world. At this juncture, as witness to science's capacity to transform and when allied with technology destroy the ways of life anthropology has been committed to study, the anthropologist could not possibly have viewed science in the same light as those for whom it had become an administrative and technological enterprise. As scientist the anthropologist has shared in the process of enlightenment, of expanding the scope of the rational. As ethnographer, however, he is disposed to resist it, valuing for science and man ways of knowing that are traditional, unique, sacred, and irreplaceable.

The five essays in this volume stand as exemplary models of anthropological reflection. Each points in a different direction while working through fundamental themes that define the discipline. Each is an expression of leadership, elaborating a method or model for doing good anthropology. Together they pose fundamental questions which we have sought to examine with reference to two of the most influential historians of science in our time. Doing this, certain obvious questions arise: Will anthropology ever have the unity that science is thought to need, according to Kuhn? Can a science which in its most fundamental activities requires re-enculturation in a foreign culture ever have the regard for western notions of scientific unity that are characteristic of other disciplines? Probably not. Yet regard for the methods of science and the value of unifying theory is fiercely strong in anthropology, as these essays demonstrate so well. We leave it at that.

Notre Dame is honored in having the profound and often eloquent spokesmen represented in this collection participate in the inauguration of a process of inquiry that will continue beyond our time. In the fusion of the intellectual and religious tradition that initiated the first universities of western culture with the disciplinary tradition through which western culture came to understand the non-west, possibilities are opened that one can now only imagine. Those who will develop these opportunities in decades to come have in these essays a record of significant thought in the eighties, and they will surely measure the quality and direction of their scholarship against the anthropology they find here. As they read these essays, and reread them, and probe further into the life-time works of Fox, Bennett, Turner, Harris, and Wolf they will be reminded that anthropology–science or humanity–probing the many dimensions of humankind, or looking back at the West from the perspective of its periphery, has a special role to play in each age, has questions to ask which are uniquely its own, and has understandings to offer which only it can provide. Though the explanations of human survival it generates are ever tentative and open to polemic, they are part of the wisdom that man lives by. Now joined to this discipline and its errand, Notre Dame affords a setting like no other where the dialogue can be continued, the polemic intensified, and the wisdom shared.

REFERENCES

Foucault, Michel. 1973. *The Order of Things: An Archaeology of the Human Sciences.* New York: Random House.

Geertz, Clifford. 1983. *Local Knowledge: Further Essays in Interpretive Anthropology.* New York: Basic Books Inc.

Kuhn, Thomas S. 1970. *The Structure of Scientific Revolutions.* 2nd ed. Chicago: University of Chicago Press.

Langer, Susan K. 1942. *Philosophy in a New Key.* New York: Mentor Books, New American Library.

The Disunity of Anthropology and the Unity of Mankind: An Introduction to the Concept of the Ethosystem

ROBIN FOX

It was with real pleasure that I accepted the honor of initiating the Department of Anthropology at Notre Dame. I have, however, the proverbial bad news and the good news. The bad news is that I want to argue that we do not need more departments of anthropology. The good news is that I would also like to argue that if we have to have more, then they should be in Catholic universities. This has to do with a complicated argument about original sin, innate ideas, and the downfall of empiricism. I wanted to call this talk "Putting sin back in." I was told that this would be an inappropriate and embarrassing subject at a Catholic university, where they prefer to think they are just like everyone else in the academic world. Contrariwise, I would argue that given the state of the academic world, one of the few things such institutions have going for them is that they are Catholic. And I say this as an unrepentant Protestant agnostic. (I stress *Protestant* agnostic because Catholics who become agnostic are different. They tend to be rather sad and troubled about it. Protestants, as is their wont, tend to be insufferably self-righteous.) But there it is. Since you want to be like everyone else, you'll never know why you are the potential *salvator anthropologiae,* you will only discover why you are superfluous. So be it.

I must start, then, by confessing a certain ambivalence. It is no secret that I have opposed the rapid expansion of anthropology over the last two decades—even though I have been a not inconsiderable beneficiary of that expansion. So it is obviously hard for me to sing songs of praise to the opening of yet another department. I do not share the view of academic subjects as growth industries. To heed most of my colleagues would be to conclude that quantity was all, and that the army of unemployed Ph.D.'s now marching out into the real world represented a measurable loss to the discipline. But where is it written that we should have been producing them in the first place? How do we measure the costs and benefits? By the number of Ph.D.'s produced, they reply—not always seeing the circularity of this reasoning.

The "expansion" of anthropology, I would argue, came at a most unfortunate time. It came at a time when anthropology was sadly fragmented into specializations and stuck in an ideological quagmire. To this unfortunate mix we must add the structure and expectations of American academic life. The individualistic and entrepreneurial nature of the American academy, where success is measured by weight of publications, leads to the expectation of numerous and, God help us, *original* publications by each and every one. The gloomy population theories of Thomas Malthus used to be answered by the assertion that with every hungry mouth God sent an active pair of hands. Unfortunately, in the academic world, with every active mouth God sends but one indifferent brain. Einstein used to maintain, whimsically, that he only ever had *one* original idea. Most of us don't rise to that. This doesn't mean that good work can't be done; it can be and it is. It means that rather than it being consciously done as part of a collective, corporate activity in which it is seen as a small but necessary contributing part, it has to be exalted into an individual "achievement," to legitimize promotion and enhance status. The best way to do this, given an indifferent intelligence, is to specialize like crazy. The smaller the intellectual pond, the bigger appears the academic fish.

This sounds harsh, and I am certainly not suggesting anthropology is unique in this respect. But while in some disciplines there might be a positive advantage to the proliferation of specializations, this hit anthropology at a very bad period. The last thing we needed was specialization. For anthropology was not in that state of development where healthy specialization had begun; it was simply fragmented through a failure to coalesce into a unified science. Specialization is only healthy within a science unified by an accepted general theory (or paradigm, as it has become fashionable to call it). The life sciences, unified by the theory of natural selection, can specialize merrily with profit. They can argue about and modify the theory itself without damaging consequences. Anthropology, however, is unified only by a concern with culture, not by a general theory of it. Any disputes about this subject matter, turning as they do on points of definition and ideology, are preludes to even further fragmentation. The affluent hordes of new anthropologists seized on each new fragment and elaborated it. The result is the present chaos and darkness over which Notre Dame is brooding like the biblical dove. Can order be brought out of this chaos? Perhaps, but certainly not in seven days.

One of the consequences of this recent history is that most anthropologists have given up the idea of a unified anthropology and have accepted the necessity of fragmentation as a virtue. Anthropology simply becomes an employment convenience—a useful fiction that administrators accept as valid and which provides a suitable cover for intellectual espionage. Departments go on stubbornly appointing the quota of linguistic anthropologists, symbolic anthropologists, physical anthropologists, archaeological anthropologists, mathematical anthropologists, medical anthropologists, applied anthropologists, ecological anthropologists, primatological anthropologists, psychological anthropologists, feminist anthropologists, cognitive anthropologists, structural anthropologists, marxist anthropologists, urban anthropologists, and, in California, para-normal anthropologists. They do this knowing that they are simply housing these people in the same corridor and with no real expectation that they will do more than preach to each other. Their professional organization, which started as a learned society and was one of America's most distinguished, has now become simply a trade union and lobbying operation for all those who call themselves "anthropologists" and pay their dues. They have nothing left in common, it seems, except the prospect of unemployment. They are a vested academic interest to be protected, not a collegiate body which exists for learned disputation. The ultimate irony is that a group of concerned members have now founded a new society *within* the American Anthropological Association called the "Society for Cultural Anthropology"! It's that bad.

So much for fragmentation and the institutional problems. I have alluded also to the "ideological quagmire" and this is, of course, a contributor to the fragmentation. I have argued elsewhere and at length on this subject and it gets dangerously close to original sin, so I shall merely summarize here.

Anthropology is an heir to the humanist, empiricist, liberal tradition that started with the Renaissance, coalesced in the Enlightenment, and became a serious political force in the nineteenth century. Darwin added fuel to this position; he did not, as is often wrongly assumed, start it for anthropology. It is indeed curious today to see Darwinism so freely associated with reaction, when in its origins it appeared as a revolutionary materialism threatening the whole Establishment. But anthropology was ambivalent during its formative period. In England it split apart on the slavery issue: there was always a reactionary wing. In America it found itself having to take a stand on eugenics. How quickly we forget our intellectual history. How many anthropologists could give a coherent account of the once powerful eugenics movement and its alliance with the Progressive party? This presented a real dilemma to anthropology. The "split mind" I have referred to elsewhere began here. Tylor had uncompromisingly declared anthropology "a reformer's science"–particularly in its role as sweeper away of "survivals," as in religion. The Darwinian theory of evolution gave anthropology an uncompromising materialist base. Yet there was much hesitation on this score. Matthew Arnold in fact elaborated the modern concept of "culture" for the middle classes to fill the gap left by the receding tide of faith. These two notions of culture sat uncomfortably side by side: Tylor's materialistic, reformist view, and Arnold's integrative and uplifting notion of sweetness and light. Strangely, it was a view of culture more like Arnold's that prevailed in social science, although this again has not been recognized, except by George Stocking.

Anthropology had banished faith and raised the spectre of race. It had to accept evolution, and human variation was real. But how could this be reconciled with its liberal, reformist stance? Anthropology temporized. It mitigated the harshness of its potential materialism and banished the eugenicist/racist spectre by elaborating the concept of "culture" as non-genetic, superorganic, *sui generis*. Even Huxley had felt driven to make the distinction between "cosmic evolution" and "ethical evolution," and anthropology seized on this distinction to restore the uniqueness of man. In fact anthropology re-cast itself in the role of defender-of-the-faith in the uniqueness of man, and thus usurped the church which was still floundering with the concept of the "soul."

In America Kroeber elaborated the doctrine of culture as superorganic, and cultural determinism was launched. Boas sweepingly declared genetics irrelevant and invented the implicit formula:

$$\text{genetic} = \text{race} \neq \text{culture}$$

thus preserving culture from contamination and launching cultural relativism. All this happily coincided with the rise of behaviorism and this seemed to clinch the issue.

In Europe, in a related development, but one with different roots, the answer was to follow the explicit formulations of Durkheim on society and social facts. No one knows quite whether to claim Durkheim for liberalism or conservatism, and he was indeed ambivalent. He ended life as a guild socialist and admired Saint Simon. But he too was torn between his adherence to the scientific, i.e. materialist, positivist tradition, and a concern, like Arnold's, for the anarchistic consequences of the failure of traditional institutions like the church. Comte, the father of sociology, solved the problem by founding his own church. Durkheim was more subtle. His answer: society *was* God, and its members constituted a church. But this had to be phrased in positivist terms. Thus "society" became for him (as "culture" had become in America) a reality *sui generis,* to be examined scientifically through the study of social facts. These were (a) exterior to the individual, (b) general in the society, and (c) exercised constraint on the individual through the "collective conscience." Thus Durkheim's political concerns, and the supposedly positivistic science of society, ended in a kind of sociological mysticism. Society was reified, and Durkheim, in his eagerness to carve out a piece of reality for his science, consigned psychology and biology to the individual, producing his basic equation:

$$\text{individual} = \text{biological} \neq \text{social}$$

If we put the two formulae together, then we get:

$$\text{individual/biological/genetic/racial} \neq \text{social/cultural}$$

This became the ideological linchpin of the social sciences. And for sociology it was not so bad. But for anthropology it created the schizophrenic situation to which I have alluded. For anthropology's distinctiveness lay in its grounding in the theory of physical evolution. The ideological formula, however, sundered this from the study of culture/society.

While we are on the concept of culture, it is worth noting that Boas, Kroeber, and Kluckhohn, for example, were particularly influenced by the German formulation of the idea which had its origins in Hegel and the rise of nineteenth-century nationalism. This was clearly more influential than either Tylor or Arnold (although Arnold was not himself uninfluenced by it). Its clearest expression was probably in the work of the German Romantic Nationalist, Herder. It is ironic then to follow the fortunes of the idea in American anthropology, for one of its major consequences was the doctrine of cultural relativism: each culture was an entity unto itself, understandable on its own terms, judged only by its own standards. This was conceived as a liberal onslaught on the racists and eugenicists. Genetics was not responsible for cultural differences, culture was. Papa Boas trained various attractive young ladies at Columbia to go out and pursue this, and they dutifully did so. With Benedict it was transparent, and that Mead was more influenced by ideology than ethnography has been recently demonstrated by Freeman (although to her credit she acknowledged this herself). Cultural relativism attacked the twin sins of "ethnocentrism" and "racism," and it became another fixed dogma that this was the *only* answer possible. In effect, this "answer" played right into the hands of the very ethnocentrism it sought to combat. It said that *every* culture had the right to be ethnocentric. What it was attacking was European ethnocentrism, not ethnocentrism as such.

The real answer to the problem they were addressing—as to all problems of the growing social sciences—was of course "species-centricism," if we can coin a phrase: Marx and Feuerbach's "species being"; and the precious store of variation. The tragedy is that anthropology by its very nature as a distinctive science, that is, by its commitment to Man's biological being through the study of his evolution, was the perfect science to insist on this. It threw away the chance. The ideological and methodological traps it set itself with the Durkheimian and Boasian formulae led in the opposite direction. The steady, and at times hysterical, attempts to separate the social and the biological have eroded that special position, erected a new dogma, and fragmented a promising science. Cultural anthropology, with its rampant doctrine of cultural relativism, is in fact a bastard child of German Romantic Nationalism. As such, it is paradoxically closer to the racism and fascism it fears than is a biologically based science, whose basic tenet is Washburn's empirically established position that all human races share 97% of their physical traits in common.

That piece of bald assertion makes for a natural break and gives me the opportunity to go from complaint to construction. I have in several places taken on the culturalist paradigm. I have argued that "categorical thinking" in Man does not separate him from the natural order: that his tendency to classify the world and then act on it in terms of this classificatory re-definition is in itself an evolved natural function that is perfectly explicable as such. I tackled this at the heart of the issue–kinship categories. I have also argued that the much vaunted tendency to taboo that which does not fit established categories has also a natural source and a natural function explained by the evolution of the brain. I shall return to the latter point, but let me take on the issue of "individual *vs.* social" and "biological facts *vs.* social facts" from another angle.

The only real opposition to relativism has come from those anthropologists interested in universals of culture. But the majority of these were themselves cultural determinists. The closest they came to a notion of culture as biology was the doctrine of the "psychic unity of mankind" –itself developed in opposition to diffusionism. Thus, if similar institutions or traits appeared in all societies, it was because of standard human responses to similar problems.

They didn't want to take it further than that, and those like Wissler who insisted that the logic of this was that cross-cultural uniformities were "in the genome" were politely dismissed as cranks. Much of the weakness of this school lay in the difficulty it had in defining the units by which to measure universals. Very often, as in the case of "the nuclear family" the question was begged by definition. In other cases the proposed universals were so vague—"a system of social control"—as to be simply part of the definition of social order itself. Almost all attempts concentrated on what linguists came to call "substantive" universals. And the parallel search by linguists had some important lessons: the search for substantive universals seemed barren; if there were universals they were at the level of *process*.

Geertz has been lauded for having given the death blow to the search for universals. His argument: the "universal" capacity that distinguishes man is his capacity to learn culture; thus when we see people displaying the unique behavior of their particular cultures we are in effect witnessing the universal. Thus we can forget the problem of universals and get down to the real business of examining the particular cultures. A neat argument that slips in relativity by the back door and allows anthropologists to continue business as usual. No wonder they like Geertz.

But while it is the truth and nothing but the truth, it is not the whole truth, because the acquisition of culture is not arbitrary. Geertz's formula does not dispose of the question: Why are cultures acquired in the way they are and not some other way—or infinitely different ways? They may be unique at the level of specific content—like languages—but at the level of the *processes* there are remarkable uniformities—like language again. Geertz wants to confound the varied manifestations of the processes with the processes themselves. Thus each outcome of a universal process can look very different. But it is nowhere written that universal processes should have identical outcomes; in fact it is in the nature of such processes that they should *not.*

This is true even at the level of plants. It is one aspect of the difference between genotype and phenotype and the same genotypic processes can have widely varying phenotypic outcomes. But—and here I appeal to structuralism, that perfect scion of the house of Durkheim—if the reality lies at the level of the process, then we still have a task to perform, discovering those species-specific universal processes. In linguistics it has been realized that this is the case, and while disputes abound concerning the processes of universal grammar, no ones seems seriously to dispute that this is where universal features must be found.

What then of the nature of the process? This is where I believe the search for universals ties in with the problems presented by the Boas/Durkheim formulae. Let me try it this way: it was correct to emphasize the reality of the social collectivity as more than the sum of the individuals and their actions; it was wrong to insist that this collectivity could not be biological in nature. It was correct to say the collectivity could not be reduced to the sum of its individuals, but wrong to assign the individual to the biological sphere and cut off society and culture from their biological roots. It was a mistake to assume that the biological basis of local variations could only arise directly from genetic, i.e. racial sources.

Curiously, what Durkheim's position leaves us with is the opposite of what was intended. His position was resolutely opposed to utilitarian individualism; but in insisting that "the individual" had a biological reality that separated it from "the social" it perpetuated and hardened the distinction it sought to overcome! The individual (or the organism) had a hard reality of its own in its biological facts, while society had an insubstantial reality in its social facts.

There had been the possibility of a different, if related, position, but it came from the idealist philosophers who were anathema to positivist scientists and later, curiously, tainted with the charge of reaction, militarism, and racism that we have seen backfire onto the relativists. Bradley in 1876, for example, argued brilliantly that society was the reality and "the individual" an abstraction. Foreshadowing G. H. Mead and even Goffman he saw the individual entirely as the product of his social milieu, as a reflection or refraction of his society. It sounds very Durkheimian, but with this difference: Bradley did not then make the error of assigning society to a non-biological sphere. He caught perfectly Darwin's point that society existed in nature: it pre-dated the appearance of man on earth. It was an evolutionary, biological phenomenon. "The social" therefore could not be divorced from "the biological." (Durkheim's mentor Espinas had made the same point but this was not taken up by the pupil.) Crudely, we can put Bradley's formula:

$$\text{social} = \text{biological} \neq \text{individual}$$

The individual however is not assigned to a different sphere as in Durkheim: the individual does not exist; it is an abstraction from the social. Strictly speaking, then, the formula is:

$$[\text{social (individual)}] = \text{biological}$$

(It is true that Durkheim eventually had to declare that the social was "natural." But this was to extricate himself from his own logical difficulties, not a premise of his system.)

How does this apply to process and universals? I have argued that the natural heirs of Bradley and Darwin were the ethologists since they developed the idea of the evolution of social behavior. The restriction here is that they concentrated almost exclusively on communicative behavior and saw it as expressing states of emotion (following Darwin). Behavior is more complex than this, especially in higher animals, and we needed among other things (like cybernetics) the corrective of ecology to supplement the ethological position. The ecologists also have the advantage of being concerned directly with system and process—particularly feedback systems—and this is where we have to look for universal, systematic processes.

To this we shall return, but first a small footnote, which will lead us onwards. It is objected that ethologists deal with universal social behavior in a species—"species-specific behavior." This is "the social" at the level of the species. Durkheim, however, was speaking of "the social" at the level of particular societies or cultures. If "the social" is biological, this argument goes, then the only "local" basis for it is racial; i.e. local genetic variation. Not so. This assumes a very crude kind of genetic determinism to which no geneticist would subscribe. Again, Durkheim was also speaking of general social processes, but even at the local level, as we have seen, societies and cultures can be seen as particular manifestations of general processes. If we add the ecological context to species processes of communication, then there is room for an enormous variety of such manifestations without invoking genetic variation as a basis. Its effects could at best be trivial in any case. The total mix of behavior and ecology needs a name, and "culture" is too loaded and overworked. Following the ecological usage which describes the object of study as the "ecosystem," I propose that we are looking for basic processes in the "ethosystem": the total feedback system involving general species propensities and ecological subsystems.

Variation in these can arise in many different ways but from the same underlying processes. It is interesting in this respect to turn to Wittgenstein who supposedly solved the problem of universals in philosophy with his doctrine of "family resemblances." Thus within a family, like the Churchills for example, there is a definite "Churchill face"; quite recognizable as in some sense "the same," but which on examination reveals no one feature in common to all faces. This was the problem with substantive universals. If one of them failed to turn up in even one society, it failed as a universal. But there is conceivably a *process* at work which could generate a universal and quite predictable *pattern* in which *no one feature appeared in all cases.* The following figure illustrates this.

Figure 1: *Wittgenstein*

	A	B	C	D	E	F
1	x	x	x	x	x	
2	x	x	x	x		x
3	x	x	x		x	x
4	x	x		x	x	x
5	x		x	x	x	x
6		x	x	x	x	x

The numbers are traits or features, the letters societies or cultures. No two societies are the same at the substantive level, but there is clearly a "family resemblance": a process is at work generating this pattern. I think, for example, that the elusiveness of the nuclear family or the oedipus complex as universals can be dealt with in this way. Taken as substantives they fail, but if one takes the component bonds and a theory of the bonding process, then one can see how the process generates the patterns and this would include a theory to explain why in particular instances certain bonds were *not* activated for certain purposes, hence the gaps. Thus their absence would not mean an abandoning of universals, quite the contrary: the nature of the process would explain the distribution; it would be the process that was universal. I have described such a process at length elsewhere, so I shall not dwell on it here.

Another pattern could occur on the "Guttman scale" model. In this there may indeed be common substantial elements, but very few. However there is a high degree of predictability concerning the presence or absence of related elements. Again, this is because of the nature of a universal process which operates quite predictably but does *not,* by its very nature, produce the same list of substantial elements in all cases. It is illustrated as follows:

Figure 2: *Guttman*

	A	B	C	D	E	F
1	x					
2	x	x				
3	x	x	x			
4	x	x	x	x		
5	x	x	x	x	x	
6	x	x	x	x	x	x

Here, for example, if a society (A) has a trait (1) we can predict it will have traits (2) through (6). If it does not have (1), but has (2), then it will also have (3) through (6), and so on: the standard Guttman pattern. The pattern of distribution of traits in male initiation procedures seems to follow this scheme, with the only common element being seclusion of the boys (6), and the trait (1) being severe genital mutilations. Ritualized avoidance shows a similar pattern, and with the development of multidimensional scaling techniques we are in the way to understanding how such patterns relate to each other in complex ways. What we have lacked have been theories that would tell us what processes generated the patterns. Now that we are no longer cut off from biology, and now that we know that the social is biological, we can proceed in this direction.

If the processes of the ethosystem which generate these patterns are to be understood, we have to overcome the problems posed by the "individual *vs.* society" and "organism *vs.* environment" dichotomies that are the legacy of Durkheim and cultural determinism. We have to understand that *the reality is the system,* and that "organism" and "society" are abstractions from it. Ecology and ethology both discovered this and we should learn from them.

For ecology the system is the total feedback relationship involving all the biota and resources of an econiche. For ethology the system is the set of action patterns contained in the gene-pool of a species as these are manifested in local situations. In each case there is a concrete "collectivity"–a biological collectivity–and "individuals" and "organisms" represent points in the feedback system. Only for certain analytic purposes should they be invoked. For other analytical purposes they are not relevant.

Thus we often hear in social psychology of the importance of *context* and how it impinges on the organism. Context should really be regarded as a *state of the system*, which can ignore the individual-social (or any similar) dichotomy. Once the initial state has caused an organism-environment interaction, the distinction rapidly breaks down. Once the system is set up it becomes totally recursive and you can "start" at any point in the system. The underlying reality then is the process that generates the system, not the analytically separable points of the system. Thus the organism has an output which modifies the environment; the organism-modified-environment then reacts back on the organism; the resultant organism-modified-by-the-organism-modified-environment reacts back on the organism-modified-environment . . . and so on. Reduced to a formula this is easier to see:

$$O > E(OmE) > O(OmEmO) > OmE(OmEmOmE) > OmEmO(OmEmOmOmEmOmE) > \ldots$$

The simplest process that illustrates this is the interaction of resources, digestion, and growth. But if we include the *social* environment, then the same recursive model becomes true for social behavior. Intelligent action by an organism is easily enough assimilated. With the evolution of a large prefrontal cortex concerned with future plans and strategies, and with increased memory storage, input from the environment (memory) has itself been selectively scanning the environment for further such input. Again, after a hypothetically necessary initial state, the distinction becomes for most purposes irrelevant. This is the outcome Durkheim wanted, in a way, but not by this route. It would certainly suit Bradley's model, however. (See addendum.)

Let us take an example from ecology which will illustrate one way in which a Durkheimian definition of social facts can apply perfectly to a sturdy biological fact—the biomass. This is the total amount of organic material in a population and can be simply expressed by weight. Thus a human population on a small island could weigh, say, a total of 10,000 lbs. For certain analytical purposes, e.g. analyzing the carrying capacity of the island econiche (its ability to support its population) this is the operative measure. It does not matter how it is composed. And it has real consequences. If the biomass exceeds the carrying capacity then starvation results and this can radically redistribute the units of the biomass (people). The biomass is a stern regulator. It is "exterior" to the individuals, in Durkheim's sense that it was not created voluntarily from individual wills. It is certainly "general in the society" since it includes everyone, and it exercises a savage constraint. But most dramatically it is *independent of the nature of the individuals.* It could be made up of one hundred 100 lb. adults. It could be ten 300 lb. males, twenty 200 lb. females, and sixty 50 lb. juveniles. Or any such combination. It doesn't matter. The social fact of the biomass is independent of these differences, but the lives of the individuals and the structure of their social order are heavily constrained by it, and their destinies influenced by processes involving it and the resources in a recursive relationship of the kind we have explored.

Take another striking example from the theory of kin selection. Too much has been claimed for the principle of inclusive fitness as a total form of evolutionary explanation. But as Tiger and I discussed (for the social sciences) in 1969, the work of Hamilton on the evolution of altruism filled an otherwise awkward gap in natural selection theory that Darwin had recognized as such. In this area at least it remains a powerful explanatory device. But for "altruism" to evolve, as we know, behavior has to be selected which will result in maximizing inclusive fitness—the fitness not only of the individual altruist but of a critical minimum of genes identical by descent with his. If the altruistic strategy succeeds, then the genes of the altruist will spread in the population. They will, however, always be open to victimization by cheaters, and cheating strategies could also spread. There exists an equilibrium point between these two sets of genetic strategies since clearly cheaters cannot overwhelmingly outnumber altruists. The balance is known as an "evolutionarily stable strategy" or ESS. It is arrived at by a process of kin selection. Once arrived at, the individual organisms will act in accordance with the demand to maximize their inclusive fitness either as altruists or cheaters. Even in this oversimplified model, we can see again that the ESS is a true social fact with all the characteristics Durkheim ascribed. Again, "individuals" are only analytical units for some purposes. Various collectivities—the groups of genes related by descent, the population or gene pool (local), the species itself—are the real elements in the process. A whole population can here be seen as a collection of genes, and the "units" for kin selection purposes are bundles of related genes which cut across other units like organisms.

Consider one more example: the relation between hormonal states and social relationships. This has been confused by simple-minded cause-and-effect thinking resulting from the bugaboo of "determinism." Again we must think in system terms. The ethosystem here consists of an interplay, for initial analytical purposes, between organism and *social* environment; i.e. the other organisms with which it must interact. But if we are looking at hormonal states, we can "abstract out" the individual organisms and see the system as a constant distribution and redistribution within the biomass of whole-blood serotonin, testosterone, adrenalin, norepinephrine, etc. These can be seen as shifting around in certain concentrations and combinations. If we concentrate on certain "point" combinations, i.e. individual organisms, we can see that these vary with behavioral states. If we stop the system at any one time, we can see, for example, that the distribution of dominance, aggression, copulation, submission, escape, etc. are correlated with hormonal states, and that these constantly shift. Thus as one organism becomes more dominant, forcing another to submission, another to aggression, another to escape, and another to copulation, the previous balance of hormones shifts and has a different distribution. This different distribution in turn shifts the balance of social forces which in turn shifts the balance of hormones—and so on in the completely recursive manner already described. This is one way in which the biology of behavioral systems works. It is exactly like an ecological system with the society being the environment. And that is why I think the term "ethosystem" is appropriate if one includes the ecological component. But it is a bio-behavioral system. And I must stress *system.* Testosterone does not *cause* dominance or aggression, but it is necessarily implicated in the ethosystem of which these are processes. At the risk of being boring I add again that the "reality" is not the elements of the system but the processes that integrate them into a system.

One could add many other illustrative examples, like the synchronization of menstrual cycles in closely associated females that has been demonstrated in non-human primate groups, female prisons, women's dorms, and hunting bands. Such processes are social facts and biological facts; collective facts and products of evolution. They do not recognize the individual-social distinction as an absolute; it is relative to analytical purposes. For most purposes the distinction is not useful. This approach has little use for the concept of race, which is not a category well enough defined to be useful in analyzing ethosystems. Our approach puts the emphasis back on species-specific behavioral and cognitive processes, but looks at these in ecological perspective. This perspective over short runs is of course an "historical perspective," and, as we have seen, once genetic modifications have occurred over longer runs, an evolutionary perspective. Thus the analysis of ethosystems is structural, historical, and evolutionary. With its knowledge of the long-run universal processes produced by evolution, it is perfectly capable of analyzing the short-run local differences produced by history. So that particularly silly debate is circumvented. It can perfectly well handle the role of intelligent, conscious behavior in the ethosystem, and it does not therefore, thank God, require the concept of culture at all—which is as well since we cannot seem to agree on its definition.

I said I would return to the brain since I believe that many issues in anthropology can be settled eventually through a study of its mechanisms. I have elsewhere explained why I think a study of the memory mechanisms of the brain will help us understand anthropological quandaries over taboo and pollution. I can only summarize here. Douglas and Leach have argued persuasively that we regard as polluting and tend to taboo those things that offend our systems of categorical thinking. What they do not explain is *why*. I followed Winson in showing that ever more complex studies of the memory system—including the role of slow-wave sleep and REM sleep (dreaming)—have established a three year period during which long-term memories are laid down. During this period items assembled in the pre-frontal cortex are constantly "rehearsed" by being passed through the limbic system, which is also the center of emotional facilitation and control. The upshot of this is that nothing gets lodged in the long-term memory unless it has had a three year vetting by the emotional system. In Ojemann's graphic phrase, this "stamps in" the memories. The remakable conclusion is that there is nothing in the long-term memory, including our most "rational" of categories and systems of classification, that has not undergone a three year testing and validation. The categories of social classification are established on a strong emotional basis. And this basis is *physical*—actual changes in the size and functions of the synapses occur, triggered by the cell DNA, after a critical point of "rehearsal" has been passed. That is why it takes three years. It is small wonder that we react with extreme anxiety (again physically measurable) when this established category system is challenged by ambiguous items.

This has tremendous implications for our understanding of the relation between systems of classification from kinship terms through to totemism up to vast religious schemes. It makes immediate sense of Durkheim's theory of social solidarity. In traditional societies where everyone went through much the same experiences, the "collective consciousness" could be very strong because the *same* systems of emotion-laden categories would exist, *physically,* in everyone. The "collective representations" and the "individual representations" would be the same. Once society became more differentiated, then different groups would have different, or only partially overlapping, systems, and these must be in conflict. What disgusts or pollutes or even only upsets one group is not the same as in another. In a society like our own, where individuation and differentiation has reached its height, we are almost at the stage where every individual has a different physically based set of categories and anxieties. This is Durkheim's *anomie,* and it is real, physical, measurable.

The decline of social solidarity, the increase in individualistic suicide, social anomie, and the weakening of the collective conscience all follow. The role of ritual, as Durkheim saw, must change accordingly. When the experiences were uniform, the physical category systems were the same for everyone and the anxieties associated with them consequently "general in the society." Thus *collective* rituals could work, because they were therapeutic bastions against totally collective anxieties. As the process became more and more specific to the individual, the therapies had to be so tailored, until in the end each person is having a highly particularized ritual performed, or is taking drugs which specifically modify those synaptic connections we have spoken of, thus bringing temporary and artificial relief. The difference then between different states of social solidarity and the collective conscience, and the basis for our reactions of pollution and taboo, lies in the mechanisms of the brain, themselves the product of an evolution that makes sense of it all by explaining these, not as social pathologies, but as adaptational outcomes of quite understandable selection pressures–in this case of social and sexual selection pressures that have understandable social and reproductive results, lodged in the brain.

I speak here as though this approach was an accomplished fact, as Jane Austen would have said, "universally to be acknowledged." That is my little fantasy. Alas it is not, and I seriously doubt that it will be accomplished by the reform of anthropology. The ideological stubbornness and vested academic interests are too strong, and people by and large too intellectually lazy, for this to happen. Their synapses are too enlarged by now. But happen it will, even if not in anthropology. The sheer weight of evidence from the natural sciences will swamp the simple-minded ideology of social science. Soon it will be obvious even to the most recalcitrant cultural determinist that Durkheim and Boas–right as they were about many things–were essentially prescientific, and that their formulae were political adaptations fully understandable at the time but no longer binding on a better-informed generation. By that time, however, a new social science will have arisen, probably directly from natural science itself.

It would certainly be nice to think that the new department at Notre Dame might be one of the sparking points for this scientific revolution. I can only wish it well, despite my gloomy strictures. After all, in the course of this lecture I have managed to suggest a role in the *scienzia nuova* for ethnography, ethology, ecology, primatology, genetics, evolutionary theory, neuroscience, cross-cultural studies, mathematical anthropology, linguistics, history, systems theory, and the study of ritual—and I could have suggested more. It is not that any one of these is doing anything particularly wrong: it is just that the total ideology to which they are devoted is wrong. But let them all flourish, and when the ideological reformation is at last successful, Notre Dame will realize why it makes perfectly good sense to ask me to lecture on anthropology and original sin.

Addendum

When looking for a simple illustration of the positive feedback loop involved in one type of ethosystem, I invoked the relation between resources, digestion, and growth. This was intended simply to illustrate the point that a process was involved here in which "organism" and "environment" were only analytically distinguishable, since part of the "environment" was constantly being converted into "organism"—and with the production of bio-degradable excreta, vice versa. But this simple resource → digestion → growth model can be expanded to include *social* variables if certain digestive conditions hold. I am thinking here of the work of Richard Wrangham (some unpublished, but see "An Ecological Model of Female-bonded Primate Groups," *Behavior,* 75: 262–300, 1980). He has demonstrated that primate species differ in certain crucial features of their digestive systems, notably the ability to de-toxify unripe fruits, seeds, grasses, or young leaves high in tannin and alkaloids. A specific liver enzyme—urate oxidase—is responsible for this digestive ability. Wrangham argues (although I can only give a simplified version here) that these differential digestive abilities facilitate different optimal feeding strategies for secondary food sources. In particular, for those species with the enzyme, it encourages the classic maternal extended families, or female kin coalitions, that primatologists have described in such detail. I myself noted that these seemed to be associated with particular species, but did not know why this should be ("Primate Kin and Human Kinship" in R. Fox ed., *Biosocial Anthropology,* New York: Halsted Press, 1975.) This is a beautiful example because it shows that while there are "genetic," "social," and "ecological" *components,* again *the reality is the process itself*—the system/feedback-loop—and not any simple unidirectional causal relation between components. If the animals are put into an environment where these secondary food sources (the resources) are not available, then the feeding strategy will change and hence the social grouping, for example. We can envision it thus:

Figure 3

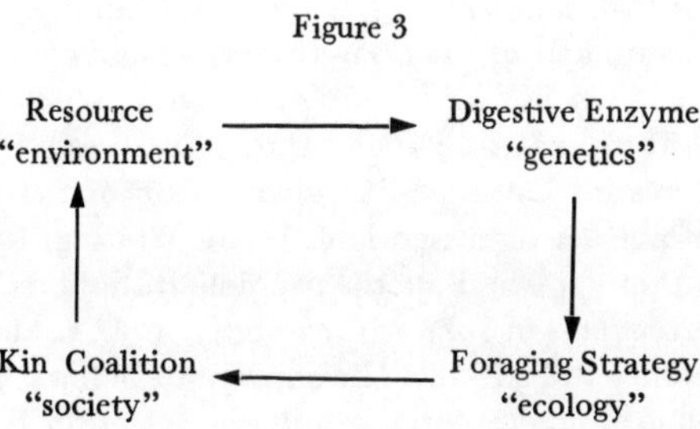

Therefore we can see that not only the growth of the organisms (which we could include in the loop under "metabolism" or some such) but an important component of their social structure is part of the continuing—and continually readjusting—feedback process. If they lack either the enzyme or the resources, primates are forced into other strategies, other maximizations, other social structures. For what is worth, *Homo sapiens sapiens,* like its cousins the Great Apes, lacks this enzyme. But that is another story.

NOTES

Since this essay covers the whole sweep of anthropology through its history, a list of references would be endless if I documented every point in detail. The classical works of Darwin, Durkheim, Boas, Kroeber, Tylor etc. referred to in the first part are all well known and available in standard editions. The work of Matthew Arnold referred to is of course his *Culture and Anarchy* (1869); the excellent commentary on this by George Stocking is in his *Race, Culture and Evolution* (Free Press: 1968). Herder's work is *Outlines of a Philosophy of the History of Man* (T. Churchill trans., 2nd. ed. 1803)—see also Stocking op. cit. for further commentary. Derek Freeman's criticism of Mead (and hence Boas) is in his *Margaret Mead and Samoa* (Harvard University Press, 1983). Clifford Geertz's treatment of the universals issue is in his collection *The Interpretation of Culture* (Basic Books, 1973), and F. H. Bradley's astonishing essay on "My Station and its Duties" in his *Ethical Studies* (Oxford, 1876). Ludwig Wittgenstein, to some people's satisfaction, settled the universals problem in his *Philosophical Investigations* (Macmillan, 1953).

For the second half of the essay readers should consult the extensive references in my *The Red Lamp of Incest: A Study in the Origins of Mind and Society* (Notre Dame University Press, 1983). Specifically, the interesting Guttman-like distribution of traits in boys' initiation ceremonies is discussed in J. W. M. Whiting, R. Kluckhohn, and A. S. Anthony, "The Function of Male Initiation Ceremonies at Puberty," in *Readings in Social Psychology*, ed. E. E. Maccoby, et al., (New York: Henry Holt, 1958). The concept of biomass is a commonplace of any ecology textbook, and kin selection has been well summarized in E. O. Wilson, *Sociobiology* (Harvard University Press: 1975), and given a sprightly and readable treatment in Richard Dawkins, *The Selfish Gene* (Oxford: 1976). Hormonal states and social status are best dealt with in *Hormones, Drugs, and Primate Social Behavior*, ed. H. Steklis and A. Kling, (New York: Spectrum Publications, 1983). See especially the work of Steklis and Kling themselves and that of McGuire and Raleigh. More work in this area, including work on humans, continues to appear almost daily. The discussion of the relations of social states to brain, memory, categories, etc. is an extension of chapter seven of *The Red Lamp of Incest* ("The Matter of Mind"), where the appropriate references can be found, especially to the ongoing work of Jonathan Winson. Readers should consult the book by Winson titled *Brain and Psyche: The Biology of the Unconscious* (Doubleday, 1985) which gives his thesis in detail. And no one should miss the extraordinary essay by Victor

Turner, "Body, Brain, and Culture" included in this volume. I quote his first sentences: "The present essay is for me one of the most difficult I have ever attempted. This is because I am having to submit to question some of the axioms anthropologists of my generation—and several subsequent generations—were taught to hallow. These axioms express the belief that all human behavior is the result of social conditioning. Clearly a very great deal of it is, but gradually it has been borne home to me that there are inherent resistances to conditioning." There follows a most brilliant discussion of the relation of the brain to culture and ritual by someone who must surely rank among the greatest of all "symbolic" anthropologists. His death was not only a personal loss for many of us, and a sad day for anthropology, but was obviously keenly felt by those of us who have been working for twenty or more years to bring anthropology round to this point of view. We can only hope that others will have as much intellectual courage as he did.

The work of the author referred to on page 24 can be found in R. Fox, "Kinship Categories as Natural Categories" in *Evolutionary Biology and Human Social Behavior,* ed. N. A Chagnon and W. Irons (Duxbury Press, 1979), and in what is an expansion of the argument of chapter 7 of *The Red Lamp of Incest,* "The Passionate Mind: Brain, Dreams, Memory and Social Categories," *Zygon* 21, no. 1 (1986): 31-46.

Anthropology and the Emerging World Order: The Paradigm of Culture in an Age of Interdependence

JOHN W. BENNETT

Introduction

In an age of social transition, the best the social sciences can do is to mark time and wait for a stable new order—assuming, of course, that a new order is on the way. Cultural anthropology built its first world view on an old order: colonialism, a system that helped preserve tribal cultures well into the era of technology and national states. What is the aftermath? Politically speaking, more nations, and more technology, and more economic interdependence. Local cultures appear to be in eclipse since much of the culture and social organization associated with high technology and advanced economic interaction is becoming universal. But cultural styles can be persistent, and perhaps we are on the threshold of an age of emerging new cultures. Or, is the next century to be one of grey homogeneity and enforced order in a massive world population? If this is the future, then what role can anthropology play? Will it serve as a reminder of the need for cultural diversity, using the past as example, or will it find new tasks to perform in the effort to establish a more humane universalism?

I focus on sociocultural anthropology since this subdivision of the discipline is most deeply involved in world transition. Archaeology and biological anthropology, both mainly oriented toward the past, have their own agenda which, if funds can be found, can be pursued indefinitely without fear of being out-moded. Sociocultural anthropology has been humanistic in instinct, but scientific in outlook. The thrust of its history has been to scientize humanism (not, I think, the reverse) and this hybrid scholarly posture has generated some curious contradictions. There is a disposition to have one's cake and eat it too, a stance which irritates both the humanities and the material sciences. Can one really make a science out of history? Despite persistent attempts to answer this question, the situation remains unclear since anthropology is caught between two successful paradigms, and by and large lacks one if its own.[1]

What is the "emerging world order" of our title? The sentence is optimistic since "emerging" implies a coming reality and "order" sounds beneficial. Optimism seems the right posture, although the writer is less so than he may appear in this paper. Besides, not all the signs of the emerging universal order are necessarily good, although Rene Dubos, a former pessimist, recently became optimistic about things (1981). We shall not discuss the pros and cons but simply present the trends as we see them and then ask what significance they may hold for anthropology's intellectual posture.

In the first and most general sense, the emerging world order would consist of the answers to a series of questions affecting human survival; that is, certain answers would mean that the world is moving toward a broad uniformity and a universal self-awareness. Thus: will we learn to control war, or to find an international substitute? Will we find a way to live with the physical environment and use resources so as to reasonably maintain a sustained supply? What are the major forces in human behavior that need reform and control, and how universal are they? How does the need for greater control over human behavior square with the equally urgent question for freedom and human rights? Is culture—the proclivity of humans to create their own distinctive images of life and the world—really the most fundamental right of all, or is it the most divisive force in human behavior? Which cultures shall we save? Which must go? Must we practice triage?

At the moment there are no clear answers to these questions. At best, what we have are makeshift and often desperate compromises. The effort to create a peaceful world is mainly an effort to create mutual dependence or deterrence in the midst of general hostility. For example, there are international fund transfers, patched up welfare statism, international food relief, arms reduction conferences. Organizations to protect culture and vulnerable populations, several with anthropological participation, begin to appear in the international system: Cultural Survival, Oxfam, Amnesty International, and of course our old friend, the United Nations.

As a second definition of international order, we can list specific developments, especially the following:

1. *The increasing importance of a limited number of universal modes of communication:*
   Specifically: The spread of the English language as a world language.
   The growing importance of meta-languages, like computer languages.
   The decision-making processes of modern society.
   The use of technological media, like television, for mass communications.
   The use of economic concepts of behavior and measurement in all countries and cultures.
2. *The increasing use of conscious planning to effect social change,* as exemplified in economic and social development programs.
   As in the case of languages and media, the mode of articulation and decision-making creates its own

culture—a culture rapidly becoming international in scope. While the Third World countries—the former home of "culture"—may eventually work out their own synthesis of these pan-cultural decision patterns, there is no doubt that a universal system of interpretation and manipulation of reality is emerging.

The increasing use of economic analysis to define the conditions of society.

3. *The emergence of an intercultural "high culture,"* exemplified in the arts, communication and entertainment media, design, architecture, modes of expression.
4. *The merging of local cultures and lower levels of social organization into larger systems on a national and supra-national scale.*

   This process means interdependency on a world canvas. Complexities of the process are evident in the form of contradiction and paradox, as earlier modes of cultural expression cross-cut the new universal forms. Ideology is particularly vulnerable, especially the ideologies forged in the European crucible in the nineteenth century, and in response to the dislocation of industrialism. Who, for example, is dependent on whom? Who exploits whom? Freedom from want generates new vulnerabilities and dependencies; development favoring the locality promotes invasion of the locality by the universal system.
5. *The emergence of an international system of finance,* regulated to a degree by organizations like the International Monetary Fund, World Bank, and so on.

   The term "New International Econonic Order" was coined at the Bretton Woods Conference, which established IMF, World Bank, and other instrumentalities. International trade, banking, and foreign aid programs are now loosely coordinated by these institutions. Much remains to be done. Aside from

> this "new" international economic order, there is the "natural" international economic order. This refers to the growing interdependence of all nations on trade, finance, loans, foreign aid, transfer funds, and so on—the loose-jointed system which remains largely dominated by the capitalist West, but is increasingly subject to checks and balances as Third World nations find ways to control it.

The broad implications of these developments for anthropology are obvious. Regardless of what is happening to local cultural styles, people the world over are learning to accept common mental images of the meaning of life and the nature of human survival. All cultures are now bi-cultures; that is, whatever they may possess of their own traditional relatively isolated past, they now also share some component of international style and its media of communication and thought. This will mean that anthropologists working in a community will be identified with this international culture. They already are so identified, and in many localities the identification is a negative one. The local people reject the international culture as an imposition, or worse, as a means of depriving them of the security and stability of their traditional way of life.

Since the question of the tribal and peasant "victims" of development recently has been dealt with by others,[2] I will not engage this aspect of the problem. I shall, instead, try to deal with the professional and intellectual aspects in a series of vignettes. The first is a discussion of the concept of culture and the implications it may hold for anthropology's attempt to comprehend the emerging and changing world order. The second concerns a major process of social change associated with this emerging order, and one that anthropologists might especially examine; the relationship of local and microsocial spheres of action to macrosocial processes and entities, like the state. The third vignette deals with the role of religion—or what may turn out to be anthropology's attempt to scientize humanism.

The Paradigm of Culture

Four concepts associated with the idea of culture as it developed in American anthropology in the 1930s have important implications for anthropology's intellectual preparation for dealing with the historical present. They are: (1) The postulate that the culture is (or cultures are) *sui generis*—that is, culture is self-generating, or tends to arise outside of the sphere of awareness of the people who bear it. (2) That cultures—those historical entities manifesting particular styles of culture—are all relatively valid and equal. (3) That culture is best represented in small, geographically isolated, self-contained, subsistence-oriented human communities, which have very different styles of life and meaning. (This third concept was probably a projection of a methodological fact; most of the work of anthropologists was accomplished in communities of this kind.) (4) That contentual emphasis is on mental or expressive phenomena. This is the idea that culture consists mainly (or that the most appropriate definition *is*) of attitudes, values, preferences, and symbols.

These four concepts are basically descriptive and typological. They contain no theory of human behavior other than a simple deterministic one; humans are the creatures of their cultures, to quote Ruth Benedict.[3] The social sciences in the first quarter of the twentieth century were dominantly typological. The major effort was devoted to ascertaining the principal varieties of social phenomena and the behavior traits of individuals and groups. In this sense, both psychology and anthropology were methodologically identical: psychology defined individual behavior in the form of traits, anthropology defined culture as the traits of groups, and neither had a theory of human behavior which would explain why people did what they did in the real world of social action. Lacking such a theory, it was not possible to determine precisely how or why anything happened in social life, other than conventional tautological or deterministic explanations. Sociology was somewhat different. It had a concept of *institution* which was less concerned with traits and more concerned with the rules people actually followed—or were supposed to follow—in ordering their affairs. In the notion of "rules" there was the germ of an explanatory theory, although tautology was also apparent—institutions consist of rules people follow, and when they follow them, people create or reinforce institutions. This is not especially different from the cultural tautologies used by anthropologists, but there is one important difference. Embedded in "institution" was the idea of a collectivity—a social group of some kind interacting with itself and with others, and cognitively appraising reality. Anthropology implicitly held that the group was not the primary reality—it was the *traits* of the group, the "culture." Sociology's conceptual level allowed for greater apprehension of trans-group phenomena and larger systems of action.

Now the four concepts of culture possess definite implications for the question of how to study the historical social present, the ongoing reality of human affairs. First, the notion of culture as a *sui generis* phenomena discourages a search for causation in human actions. These actions automatically arise wherever humans might be found. The possibility that humans themselves *created* culture in a theater of social interplay was inadequately realized. The possibility that culture might be *imposed* on humans by the state or some other social entity was neglected. The possibility that cultures might be absorbed into ever-larger systems of thought and action, channelled by institutions and organizations, was only dimly perceived. The notion of *sui generis* culture was, of course, roughly appropriate for the kinds of relatively isolated, history-less societies studied by anthropologists, but even here one wonders why so little was made of the colonial process and its forceful mandates for cultural change. When these things were acknowledged, the processes were absorbed once again into abstractions: "Westernization," "modernization," "diffusion," "acculturation." Such concepts were on the whole consistent with the detached, impersonal, *sui generis* notion of culture.

The second concept of culture—the notion that all cultures are equally valid expressions of human attitudes and action—was consistent with the foregoing; culture was a natural emergent, and Nature is not subject to value judgments. The fact that some cultures might contain certain destructive forces, detrimental to the interests of their own "bearers" or to their neighbors was only dimly perceived.[4] It took the Nazi phenomenon in World War II to refute the simplistic notion of relativity and to relegate it to a routine methodological attitude to facilitate fieldwork and data analysis.

As suggested the first two concepts were perhaps outgrowths of the third—that culture arises in small, isolated, primary social groupings, and that therefore cultures differ greatly from one another. The writer considers this third concept the most valid of the lot. Still, very little was done with it in anthropology save for the work of Robert Redfield (1974). He recognized that culture arises when people have an opportunity to communicate intimately and regularly on the same set of topics. Culture, in this sense, is simply repeatedly shared experiences. In large, complex societies, shared experience is minimal or relegated to simple universals that do not penetrate below the surface of everyday participation. However valid the concept, it lacked a theory of cultural duality. The shared universals, from the standpoint of inter-group survival, are just as important as the shared experiences and symbols. In the emerging world order, they become all-important—they are equivalent to "peace." But anthropologists neglected these universals in their preoccupation with cultural diversity.

The fourth concept, the emphasis on mentalistic phenomena and associated ritual, symbols, and so on, directed the attention of anthropologists away from the socially active nature of human behavior. The possibility that values, for example, might be manipulative strategies to accomplish specific ends and not enduring ideals guiding action was poorly understood.

Together, these four concepts had the effect of directing the attention of anthropologists away from the living social reality of human affairs and back toward typology and static conceptions of social process. Let me hasten to say that the awareness that something more than cultural typology was needed began appearing in anthropology during the 1950s as anthropologists began observing the dynamism of world events and processes[5] in a world rapidly and drastically changing from the established routines of the prewar period. Thus arose the "hyphenated anthropologies" (economic, ecological, medical, etc.) in an effort to find causes in other disciplinary subject matter.

But despite the great changes, the intellectual heritage of anthropology remained closely associated with the paradigm of culture. This had several effects on the discipline's preparation to comprehend the historical present. Many of these effects are implicit in the foregoing discussion. However, and in general, it meant that anthropologists had difficulty understanding the nature of the nation state and the force of trans-group organizations. Second, it made it difficult to conceive of social process as a reality in its own right. Since there was no genuine theory of human behavior there could be little comprehension of how people used, manipulated, or rebelled against culture. Third, and perhaps most important in my view, it prevented the emergence in anthropology of a genuine theory of large systems. This was abetted by the pervasive concern with small, supposedly isolated groups of humans—geographic isolation was supposed to create vicinal isolation, hence unique cultures. Anthropology still conspicuously lacks a theory of large social collectivities or social systems. It must depend on sociology or economics for this theory (not necessarily bad of course, but perhaps we should try to do better). Finally the culture paradigm prevented consideration of a most grievous and embarrassing fact: that culture—that is the appearance of distinctive styles of thought and action in particular groups—might be a generalized behavioral proclivity counter to the best interests of mankind as a whole.

Let us examine this last proposition. The emerging world order entails an unparalleled increase in what we may call proximity, that is, the breakdown of isolation. (Isolation was never as great as ethnologists assumed, of course, but let us not pursue that here.) For the first time in modern history (roughly since the seventeenth century) world societies are in close communication with one another and thus becoming dependent on one another. The nation-state and the international economic order, implemented by development programs and the spread of communication media, permitted social groups of all sizes to become aware of their neighbors' interests and values, and to conceive, in countless ways, real or imagined, that these elements might be antithetical to their own. The result has been a rapid intensification of conflict and irreparable confrontation, nonnegotiable demands, and other alarming trends. Tribal warfare arose in Africa as the state demanded universal conformity. National warfare arose in Southeast Asia as territorial expansion became essential to the furthering of new national aims. Religious conflict arose in Ireland as external forces generated renewed prejudice and intolerance. But underneath all those manifestations of separation are forces toward conformity and unity.

Well, we see that the traditional theory of anthropology was not in a position to anticipate culture as a divisive and destructive force in human affairs, whatever other benevolent function it might have. Anthropologists have shown considerable unwillingness to accept this formulation, and one can sympathize with them. It is always difficult to accept—at least publicly—the possibility that a sacred paradigm is not only inaccurate and inadequate, but possibly even socially ominous. This is in spite of the fact that anthropologists have made significant progress in the past twenty years in accepting the nature and complexity of human behavior and the social realities it generates.

The Micro-Macro Nexus and Supra-Systems

Anthropology's confrontation with growing cultural interdependence and international communication is now in its second decade. The key phrase for some years has been "complex society." Originating in the 1950s, this term is used to designate the larger agglomerations of people, although the term really refers to one of those culture types we have already criticized. The point is that the whole world is one big "complex society" and the term makes little sense if you use it to apply to, say, a fragment of this society like an administrative district, a local government body, or a city as if it were an isolate. This habit of anthropologists to ignore real-life categories and translate them into abstract types is one of the things we are concerned about.

Granted, say anthropologists, that a growing cultural and economic interdependence characterizes the world society, there still remains a potential in human groups to evolve distinctive local styles of life ("cultures," or whatever one calls them). It is anthropology's duty to research these evolving uniques, and call them to the attention of the bureaucracies, who persistently generalize about values and motives on the model of The Culture they are most familiar with. This critique of the universalistic practices of public administration everywhere in the world is standard. It lies behind the basic criticisms of development projects in the Third World countries made by anthropologists and others. And of course there is much truth in it. But the argument does not really grapple with the fundamental issues. How can anthropologists study the emerging pancultural world order and its contradictory tendencies if they remain wedded to concepts rooted in the notion of discrete cultures? What theories are they to use? I do *not* believe that anthropology can afford to neglect the macro-social order and the global pattern of intercultural emergence. I believe that anthropology *must* be prepared to work at the macro levels, transcending its preoccupation with the micro and the local, but at the same time providing a unique synthesis of the micro and the macro because that is what is taking place anyway—however disorderly the process. This is to say that I do not follow the conventional line to the effect that anthropology can make its most important contribution by forcing the attention of bureaucrats on the novel and significant qualities of local culture, important though this may be in some contexts. This is not really a scientific venture; it is in essence a public relations campaign—a desirable one, but not a substitute for new thinking and theorizing about the direction modern society is taking.

Let us now turn to the emergence of large supra-systems composed of the interaction of microsocial or local phenomena with larger institutions, the absorption of communities into the nation, and the linkage between local societies and the national and international systems of markets and politics *via* development programs.

Among various models available for considering these matters, systems theory is perhaps the most useful. The application here will be heuristic and not formal. There are two ways to deal with it. The first is to conceive of systems as abstract social processes, subject to regularities and hence generalizable across cultures. The second is to consider systems as concrete historical entities. Such entities are held together by institutions, ideologies, economic corporations, politico-military force; a modern nation state is such a system. Over and beyond nations are international supra-systems—"the emerging world order." Immanuel Wallerstein's studies of "the modern world system" is an approach of this type (Wallerstein 1974) and it seems clear enough that in his writings economic institutions play the largest role in creating large supra-systems (cf. Fernand Braudel 1981; and of course Marx).

Actually both approaches are useful and necessary when dealing with particular issues and problems. The best extant example of a world supra-system is, as already suggested, the international economic system sometimes called the "capitalist system." (This designation is ambiguous since non-capitalist nations participate in it.) The contemporary international economic system appears to function without resorting to a return to a colonial or conquest order. Indeed, the system has prospered since the liquidation of the colonial empires, although at the cost of creating new forms of dependency. These dependency patterns are themselves one of the forms of international order we are discussing.

As dependencies are created, interaction between nations (and corporations, banks, etc.) is increased, and awareness of inequities increases as well. Then countervailing forces begin to emerge. Thus by borrowing very large sums of money from government and private sources in the First World, Third World countries do not merely accumulate debts; they come to own the banks, so to speak. Foreclosure is impossible since it would bankrupt both borrowers and lenders. Political alliances begin to respond to such new forms of interaction. The Middle East is an excellent example. The smaller states combine, separate, and combine again in a search for a defense of their interests and political leverage. "Independence" is really a matter of the stakes that any nation may have in the international economic order at any one time.

Since the order appears to prosper on the basis of a number of so-called independent states, it is evident that what has really happened is that the responsibility for social order, welfare, and profitability, once borne by empires, is now diffused across a large number of public and private organizations, many of them international in scope and nature. Consequently the nation is now a component subsystem of a larger supra-system and bears less than full responsibility for its own affairs. Great powers intervene when they feel it necessary, big corporations make deals with national governments as if they were fellow corporations, and national governments consult the World Bank or the International Monetary Fund before they make "purely domestic" decisions. To reduce the value of the U.S. dollar, the finance ministers of the industrial nations must devise an international scheme.

Among the social sciences concerned with large systems the sociological tradition was focused largely on the question of social class. Tribes, cultures, communities were seen as secondary in importance. The social class, defined as a group of people with similar opportunities or deprivations, was considered to be the basic social unit of analysis for large systems. Anthropology, on the other hand, focused on cultures, localities, and communities. The resolution of the theoretical and methodological problems arising from this difference in units of analysis was impossible so long as the issue was conceived as a purely theoretical one. History was the necessary final court of appeal. However, taking the problem at the highest level of generality—the "world systems" approach—there seems no doubt that the course of recent history under the influence of the international market system and all associated trends has seen the progressive emergence in all countries of class phenomena as increasingly assertive over against culture, ethnicity, and geography. I do not mean to imply that the cultural or ethnic phenomena are irrelevant or nonexistent —on the contrary, as countervailing forces and as symbols of identity they are a strong force—but rather that increasing numbers of people in all countries seek social advantage on the basis of their structural relationship to the political economy. Peasants in Latin America and Africa move rapidly into cash-crop production. They are willing to surrender their vicinal isolation and some of their cultural peculiarities in order to achieve a favorable place in the market system. Likewise Quebec at the moment of writing is surrendering some of its ethnic independence for practical advantage as a part of Canada. This is not a theoretical process, but a concrete historical reality; it is a "world system" phenomenon.

The crucial question concerns the nature of nationalism, and the extent to which national states will be willing and able to surrender portions of their autonomy in favor of larger combinations. Africa, for example, is presently divided into a plethora of independent nations nearly all of which were former colonial enclaves, carved out of natural and tribal systems on the basis of arbitrary political motives. Since the boundaries cut through and across natural resource parameters, leaving some "nations" with virtually no productive resources and others with an abundance, there is need for adjustment of current political boundaries in favor of others with more equitable implications for survival. The answer, of course, is regionalism, or regional economic and resource communities which distribute the necessary resources more equitably among the political units. The European Economic Community, granted its difficulties, is the prototype of the modified nationalism of the future.

All this can be very stimulating. However, supra-systems theory can be neglectful of the physical dimension of the greatest world systems; that is the impact of current events on world ecosystems and the state of the resource base. Population, food production and consumption, land degradation, environmental poisons, and the like have their own rhythms and these appear to be increasing, often at an exponential rate. While the world supra-system tends to fluctuate on the basis of adaptive power principles, the ecosystem appears to be running down. Malthusian processes operate in complex ways, not necessarily on the basis of some simple ratio of population magnitudes to available resources, but as an equation with flexible terms: it is *population size* plus *effective demand* plus the *scientific capacity to enhance,* as well as exploit, *resources.*

More useful, though less intellectually intriguing, is the synthesis of both sociological and ecological data for significant subsistence economies associated with particular world regions and biomes. I have suggested the term *socionatural system* for these entities (Bennett 1981) and a recent study by an anthropologist makes an interesting empirical attempt to analyze one (the Mormon frontier in Arizona: Abruzzi 1981). A socionatural system brings together the relevant physical resources, social resources, technology, and human needs and wants into a system of production. These systems are illumined by human values; that is, they are defined not by some environmental value, but by human purposes. This may be a fatal flaw. However, if the concept of sustained resource yield can be introduced as a check against resource abuse, this defect can be handled. The difficulty is that all such control systems are referred ultimately to human expectations or demand which are virtually unchallenged in most political systems, democratic or authoritarian.

When anthropologists use world-systems concepts in their research, the frame of reference changes radically from the community-centered approach. One starts with a large systemic entity, defines it cross-culturally, then examines a particular local case to see how participation in the system has modified, benefited, or disadvantaged the local society. A case in point is the international cooperative movement. This "movement" is an organizational template originating in the Rochdale experiment in England in the late nineteenth century (Worsley 1971). While indigenous cooperation as a pragmatic interaction pattern is as old as Homo sapiens, the modern institutionalized cooperative found in all countries, and introduced by European colonial regimes as well as the development agencies in the recent period, is a distinctive system of management and production which requires adaptation to local conditions.

The institutional cooperative contains a general ideology of mutual advantage derived from sharing scarce goods, thereby making them more readily available or more equitably distributed. This ideology is usually modified in execution, and the cooperative organization can be adapted to agricultural societies with marked inequality of ownership of productive resources. Thus, the co-op does not necessarily solve structural problems; indeed, like other developmental interventions, it may worsen them. However, for those groups who can benefit from cooperative organization, the instrumentality produces distinct gains. Cooperative organization also contains strong universalistic, rational-legal, and functionally specific elements, requiring accurate record-keeping, appropriate distribution of surpluses, equitable distribution of necessary factors of production, and intelligent dealings with outside agents of the market system. On the other hand, since the cooperative is also a local organization, it also can serve to protect indigenous cultural patterns and values against invasion by alien perspectives and practices. Such processes constitute the focus of the growing anthropological interest in co-ops in developing countries. It constitutes a good example of the use of large-system constructs to guide anthropological research on micro-macro issues.

If the examination of world order phenomena of the type we are discussing must proceed on the basis of systems theory and other macrosocial frames, then it must be acknowledged that anthropology is not well equipped to engage in it. In order to participate in research of this kind, anthropology must borrow the insights and methods of other disciplines. But anthropologists can offer some things of their own—in particular, the way the mental life of indigenous and local populations may influence their interactions with the outside world.

The most important anthropological approach to this

effort concerns the adaptational nexus: the way local people cope with external influences, and how they may strive to modify these forces in Third World countries. The rate of failure of development projects is high, and most of these failures can be attributed to the failure of planners and technical aid specialists to understand the full context of local responses to intervention. Economic thinking is based on assumptions of cross-cultural universality of certain reactions, like the desire for more return on one's labor. The possibility that this is not always appreciated or envisaged, or that local social arrangements might be jeopardized by its achievement, has been seriously neglected. Often the point is understood intellectually by the development planners, but they must officially ignore it because the plan, or the government objectives, take precedence. Anthropologists are now active in research on more local participation and autonomy in development planning (e.g., Ralston et al., 1981—a study commissioned by USAID).

Individual motives, or the motives of people in social systems, rarely conform to simple paradigms of social behavior. The tendency to assume they do is a proclivity of technical experts in urban-based institutions without first-hand knowledge of local communities and their cultures. This failing is itself a micro-macro issue and deserves independent study by anthropologists. Contributions in this area have been made by development anthropologists and these constitute one of the genuine achievements of applied anthropology—a contribution not fully appreciated by the academic fraternity. However, more often than not these contributions have issued from *critiques* of the development process rather than as products of intimate participation by anthropologists in the projects. It has been singularly difficult to incorporate basic anthropological research findings in development, largely for practical reasons. The amount of time required for an adequate anthropological study of local sociocultural conditions affecting project acceptance is usually longer than the organizational time-frame of the project itself. In addition, the recommendations made by the anthropological team-member are often couched in elliptical and qualified language; they are not specific enough to permit incorporation in a specific project design. Anthropologists need to learn how to make more carefully focused and sharply worded studies of intervention and its social matrix. They also need to be more specific about cause and effect sequences in human behavior.

In addition to the study of sociocultural factors influencing project acceptance there is a need for anthropological work on the problem of effective size or magnitude of productive processes. Attempts to merge local production systems in larger market-based entities based on Euro-American models have also not met with outstanding success, and development specialists have shown considerable interest in recent years in alternative arrangements which preserve the smaller, indigenous-technology systems. These systems have proven to be remarkably efficient users of available physical and social resources, even though their productive magnitudes are not always in conformity with externally set standards and goals. Anthropologists are engaged in research on the technical dimensions of these local systems; "cultural ecology" is giving way to more sophisticated studies of energy utilization and productive efficiency under substantively rational conditions. These can function as a needed corrective to the unrealistic goals of the development programs.

Aside from these practical dimensions, the anthropological inquiry into micro-macro relationships has a scholarly importance. Rural sociology, which grew up under the aegis of the North American and European agricultural establishment, has not understood the need for an examination of the rich social matrix of the local-external relationships in the developed societies, let alone the emerging national societies of the Third World. A new "rural anthropology" is needed and only anthropologists can supply this need.[6] There are some excellent models such as Bruno Benvenuti's study of rural life in the Netherlands (1962). An outstanding exception to the rather perfunctory research carried on by many rural sociologists, Benvenuti's approach shows an appreciation of the cultural aspects of rural-urban interaction and the influence of the external market system. In broader perspective, S. H. Franklin's studies of European "peasantry" in transition to a new pan-European market agriculture (1969) illustrate the profitable results that can be obtained when one views the agriculturalists of a continent as intelligent beings who cope with changing macrosocial forces and are willing to make trade-offs with their own institutions in the process.

Religion, Anthropology, and the World Order

As we all know anthropology is a product of the secular revolution in social thought: the roots in Darwinism, utilitarianism, social democracy, and other doctrines are obvious. But paradoxically, anthropology, alone among the social sciences, has displayed the greatest willingness to perform research on religious phenomena. It is true that most of this research was accomplished in tribal societies with their private, indigenous beliefs and rituals, but nonetheless anthropologists displayed a keen awareness of the importance of transcendent belief systems in human behavior and experience.

But another paradox emerges. Despite this awareness, anthropologists, due largely to the persistence of cultural relativity doctrines, have not displayed much adherence as individuals to any particular faith. They are in a permanent quandary; as students of the devout, they cannot be devout themselves. Compartmentalization is probably a dominant mode. More explicitly, while anthropologists have appreciated the need for ordering principles in culture, they have not found it posssible, at least as a group, to decide which set of ordering principles might be suitable or desirable, other than to sanction any existing, "functional" set.

It is now commonplace to read that the world needs a new faith, a new consensus, a new commitment to belief, a new morality. Few use the term "religion" but in effect that is what is meant. The emerging world order is being fabricated crudely and roughly out of pragmatic accommodations; the question is whether we need a spiritual and expressive unity as well. If so, which one shall we choose? Or for our own case, which anthropologist shall we choose as leader? Ruth Benedict, who wrote possibly the best short piece on tribal religion (1938); Robert Redfield, whose concept of "great tradition" defined religion as a civilizational ordering principle (1956); Roy Rappaport, who saw religion as an ecological ordering of man-Nature relationships (1971)? Is religion the same as Talcott Parsons's (1951) "universalistic patterns"?

Whatever intellectual exegesis one selects, one fact is clear: as the world order emerges, there is a requirement for a universal tradition or ordering principle. As things stand, the only one we have is the international market system, which confers unity of a sort, but which fails to connect this material unity with the moral order. Moreover, this material unity violates the ecological principle of human existence. Our fate is bound up with the earth's. We are not the earth's master, but its manager, required to sustain the yield of its finite resources.

It is the nature of moral orders to rest on belief, not on rational explication. Raoul Naroll has recently published a book with the title *Moral Order* (1983) which appears to consist mainly of techniques to determine what people believe in cross-culturally. The book takes cultural and moral pluralism for granted and proceeds to establish the most general agreements statistically, with a considerable intellectual apparatus derived from systems theory, complete with cybernetic principles. Here the "moral order" turns out to be mainly a respect for feedback. If you perform one action in society there will be a corresponding reaction in the economy, and so on. The problem of interdependency is visualized as a mechanical problem or a matter of cognition. Belief is a datum, but not a conviction; the world is not saved by a new religious faith, but by attention to cause and consequence. Ingenious as this may be, it does not address itself to the basic problem, which is that a moral order is rooted in belief—conviction—in the rightness of the world and the ability of humans to redress imbalances through adherence to an ideology. Ideology in general may be discredited, but its basis in human behavior remains firm. People still need to believe.

Moreover, belief is transcendent. It is not to be found in rational persuasion of action and consequence. The great religions produced peace of mind not because they provided solutions, but because they taught humans to accept their lot as best they could. In this sense, religion is the only means we have to control rising expectations—expectations which exceed the capacity of social systems to sustain them.

Expectations are material and secular; they contain no built-in controls. This may be the root of the "environmental" problem. Humans have lost their capacity to control their attack on nature by principles which transcend individual wants. Hence Garrett Hardin (1980) and others have insistently spoken of the need for a new "environmental ethic," a new religion which defined the role of humanity *vis a vis* a finite world and its place in the universe. But one does not create religions; they *emerge* out of fear, love, passion, and even hatred. And they are emerging everywhere, albeit heavily politicized. Great, universal religions have all arisen out of hare-brained local cults, plus charismatic leadership. Something is stirring, of that there is no doubt. What can and should anthropology do about it?

Well, they will for some time simply continue to study these emerging religions. I think they should study them more than they do; certainly the work cannot do any harm, and it may do some good. Anthropologists should make good on their tradition of taking religion seriously, relativistic or not, as the case may be. What is the state of our preparation for this work?

Sociocultural anthropology today seems to be divided into two main styles of work: those which emphasize what I have called the "instrumental" side of human existence, now and in the past; and on the other hand, the expressive or "interpretive" mode, which is concerned with the symbols and meanings of human existence to be found in various cultures (Bennett 1976). This is, of course, simply a specific version of the basic duality of modern thought: science on one side, religion on the other. It is here where anthropology betrays its participation in the dilemma of the whole modern age and the emerging world order: to obtain knowledge, one must eschew belief. But it is increasingly clear that this is the root of all our evils, however one construes it.

Anthropology has a mission. It needs to explore human existence as a combined endeavor; the synthesis of the material and the spiritual in a search for some larger ordering principle, or in more secular language, a new civilization. Is this to be the "post-industrial" or "post-civilization" society that Boulding (1978) and others have been proposing? I do not know. Are ethnic cultural traditions to become the new version of belief and commitment? I do not know. I only know that we should try to find out, to unite the instrumental and the interpretive themes of anthropological effort, and perhaps, who knows, find something to believe in ourselves.

NOTES

1. The exact meaning of the term "paradigm" is difficult to determine. Certainly "culture," however it may be defined, can be considered a paradigm for part of its period of popularity since it served as a frame for organizing data required in professional activities. However, in another sense, anthropology lacks a paradigm since "culture" was never adequate as a tool for organizing all of the data from the many sub-fields of the multi-discipline. Stocking (1968, 8) is usually cited as the first to suggest that anthropology is "pre-paradigmatic." The term is Thomas Kuhn's, who felt that the behavior sciences in general lacked a central paradigm (1970).

2. The "victim" sobriquet is a buzzword and lacks intellectual authority. Works using the concepts are on the fringe of the discipline in the sense that they are used primarily as public relations documents or secondary texts in undergraduate courses. There is an important element of truth in them since tribal and peasant peoples have been the targets of imposed change, and often presumed benefits have not materialized. The issue is extremely complex, and perhaps the main factor is the need for local populations to accept changes as a phase of a national development program or as part of a larger systematic transformation, which implies a sacrifice of some kind, so that other sectors of the population can benefit. For examples of the victimization theme, see Bodley 1982 and Davis 1977.

3. Benedict, *Patterns of Culture* (1934, 3). There is an argument as to just what Benedict meant here. The phrase, taken literally, implies that humans are mechanical dolls activated by outside cultural forces. Since Benedict wrote in evocative language the phrase more likely implies that when humans grow up in a particular social milieu, they naturally take on elements of the ideas and lifeways of that milieu. However, Benedict never investigated the individual's response to cultural patterns; deviance and despair were not part of her interests.

4. The point was made in a paper by a philosopher published in the *American Anthropologist* (Williams 1947). Williams was concerned that "Anthropology for the Common Man"—the Penguin Publication of *Patterns of Culture*—would be misinterpreted as a plea for considering social evils, like Nazism, as culturally relative, hence acceptable. In general, I believe that the decline of the paradigm of culture as the key concept in anthropology can be dated from the appearance of this paper. Jules Henry's most publicized book bore the startling title *Culture Against Man* (1963).

5. Moves toward theoretical revision began appearing: Edmund Leach's demonstration of the political fictionality of the tribe in his book on Burma (1954); R. Mac. Adams' pursuit of the origins of urbanism (1966); Barth's explorations of ethnicity as a means of maintaining boundaries (1969); Fallers' pioneer attempt at dealing with the nation-state (1974).

6. Not that some work has not already been accomplished such as Vidich and Bensman 1958; Bennett 1967; 1982. At the moment of writing, "micro-macro" research in anthropology shows signs of becoming a dominant theme: see Robert Netting's recent *Balancing on an Alp* (1981), which puts the micro-macro theme in a historical-ecological setting.

REFERENCES

Abruzzi, W. 1981. *Mormon Colonization of the Little Colorado River Basin.* Doctoral dissertation, Department of Anthropology, State University of New York, Binghamton, New York.

Adams, Robert Mac. 1966. *The Evolution of Urban Society.* Chicago: Aldine Publishing Co.

Barth, Frederick. 1969. *Ethnic Groups and Boundaries: The Social Organization of Culture Difference.* London: Geo. Allen & Unwin.

Benedict, Ruth. 1934. *Patterns of Culture.* New York: Houghton Mifflin Co.

———. 1938. Religion. In *General Anthropology,* edited by F. Boas. Boston: D. C. Heath.

Bennett, John W. 1967. Microcosm-Macrocosm Relationships in North American Agrarian Society. *American Anthropologist* 69:441–454.

———.1976. Anticipation, Adaptation, and the Concept of Culture in Anthropology. *Science* 192: 847–853.

———. 1981. Social and Interdisciplinary Sciences in U.S. Man and the Biosphere Program. In *Social Sciences, Interdisciplinary Research, and the U.S. Man and the Biosphere Program,* edited by E. Zube. U.S. MAB, Department of State, and University of Arizona, Tucson.

———. 1982. *Of Time and the Enterprise: North American Family Farm Management in a Context of Resource Marginality.* Minneapolis: University of Minnesota Press.

Benevenuti, Bruno. 1962. *Farming in Cultural Change.* Assen, Netherlands: Van Gorcum Co.

Bodley, John H. 1982. *Victims of Progress.* 2d ed. Menlo Park: B. Cummings Publishing Co.

Boulding, Kenneth E. 1978. *Ecodynamics: A New Theory of Societal Evolution.* Beverly Hills: Sage Publications.

Braudel, Fernand. 1981. *The Structures of Everyday Life: Civilization and Capitalism: 15th–18th Century.* New York: Harper & Row.

Davis, Shelton H. 1977. *Victims of the Miracle: Development and the Indians of Brazil.* Cambridge: Cambridge University Press.

Dubos, Rene. 1981. *Celebrations of Life.* New York: McGraw Hill.

Fallers, Lloyd A. 1974. *The Social Anthropology of the Nation-State.* Chicago: Aldine Publishing Co.

Franklin, S. H. 1969. *The Evolution of Peasantry: The Final Stage.* London: Methuen.

Hardin, Garrett. 1980. *Promethean Ethics: Living with Death, Competition, and Triage.* Seattle: University of Washington Press.

Henry, Jules. 1963. *Culture Against Man.* New York: Random House.

Kuhn, Thomas S. 1970. *The Structure of Scientific Revolutions.* 2d ed. Chicago: University of Chicago Press.

Leach, Edmund R. 1954. *Political Systems of Highland Burma.* Boston: Beacon Press.

Naroll, Raoul. 1983. *The Moral Order: An Introduction to the Human Situation.* Beverly Hills: Sage Publications.

Netting, Robert Mc. 1981. *Balancing on an Alp: Ecological Change and Continuity in a Swiss Mountain Village.* New York: Cambridge University Press.

Parsons, Talcott. 1951. *The Social System.* Glencoe, Illinois: The Free Press.

Ralston, Lenore, James Anderson, and Elizabeth Colson. 1981. *Voluntary Efforts in Decentralized Management.* Project in Managing Decentralization, Institute of International Studies, University of California, Berkley.

Rappaport, Roy. 1971. The Sacred in Human Evolution. *Annual Review of Ecology and Systematics.* 2:23–44.

Redfield, Robert. 1947. The Folk Society. *American Journal of Sociology* 52: 293–308.

———. 1956. *Peasant Society and Culture: An Anthropological Approach to Civilization.* Chicago: University of Chicago Press.

Stocking, George W. Jr. 1968. *Race, Culture and Evolution.* New York: The Free Press and Collier-Macmillan.

Vidich, Arthur J., and J. Bensman. 1958. *Small Town in Mass Society.* Princeton: University Press.

Wallerstein, Immanuel. 1974. *The Modern World System: I: Capitalist Agriculture and the Origin of the European World Economy.* New York: Academic Press.

Williams, Elgin. 1947. Anthropology for the Common Man. *American Anthropologist* 49:84–90.

Worsley, Peter, ed. 1971. *Two Blades of Grass: Cooperatives in Agricultural Modernization.* Manchester: Manchester University Press.

Body, Brain, and Culture

VICTOR TURNER

The present essay is for me one of the most difficult I have ever attempted. This is because I am having to submit to question some of the axioms anthropologists of my generation—and several subsequent generations—were taught to hallow. These axioms express the belief that all human behavior is the result of social conditioning. Clearly a very great deal of it is, but gradually it has been borne home to me that there are inherent resistances to conditioning. As Anthony Stevens has recently written in an interesting book which seeks to reconcile ethological and Jungian approaches: "Any attempt to adopt forms of social organization and ways of life other than those which are *characteristic of our species* must lead to personal and social disorientation" (italics added).[1] In other words, our species has distinctive features, genetically inherited, which interact with social conditioning, and set up certain resistances to behavioral modification from without. Further, Robin Fox has argued: "If there is no human nature, any social system is as good as any other, since there is no base line of human needs by which to judge them. If, indeed, everything is learned, then surely men can be taught to live in any kind of society. Man is at the mercy of all the tyrants who think they know what is best for him. And how can he plead that they are being inhuman if he doesn't know what being human is in the first place?"[2] One of those distinctive human features may be a propensity to the ritualization of certain of our behaviors, from smiling and maternal responsiveness onwards.

Theories of Ritualization

In June 1965, I took part in a discussion on "ritualization of behavior in animals and man" organized by Sir Julian Huxley for the Royal Society and held—perhaps appropriately—in the lecture hall of the Zoological Society of London, near the Mappin Terraces, where the monkeys revel. The "hard core" of the conference consisted of zoologists and ethologists, Huxley, Konrad Lorenz, R. A. Hinde, W. H. Thorpe, Desmond Morris, N. M. Cullen, F. W. Braestrup, I. Eibl-Eibesfeldt, and others. Sir Edmund Leach, Meyer Fortes, and I spoke up for British anthropology in defining ritual, but by no means as unanimously as the ethologists did in defining ritualization. Other scholars represented other disciplines: psychiatrists included Erik Erikson, R. D. Laing, and G. Morris Carstairs. Sir Maurice Bowra and E. H. Gombrich spoke about the ritualization of human cultural activities, dance, drama, and art. Basil Bernstein, H. Elvin, and R. S. Peters discussed ritual in education and David Attenborough shared his ethnographic films on the Kava ceremony in Tonga and land-diving in Pentecost, New Hebrides.

The nonethologists generally accepted Leach's position that "it cannot be too strongly emphasized that ritual, in the anthropologist's sense, is in no way whatsoever a genetic endowment of the species."[3] I took up no public position at that time, since I was secretly, even guiltily impressed by the ethologists' definition of "ritualization" which seemed to strike chords in relation to human ritual, summed up by Huxley as follows: "Ritualization is the adaptive formalization or canalization of emotionally motivated behavior, under the teleonomic pressure of natural selection so as: (a) to promote better and more unambiguous signal function, both intra- and inter-specifically; (b) to serve as more efficient stimulators or releasers of more efficient patterns of action in other individuals; (c) to reduce intra-specific damage; and (d) to serve as sexual or social bonding mechanisms."[4] Actually, much of Huxley's definition is better applied analogically to those stylized human behaviors we might call "communicative," such as manners, decorum, ceremony, etiquette, polite display, the rules of chivalry (which inhibit the infliction on one another of damage by conspecifics) than to ritual proper.

In various publications I have suggested that ritual was "a *transformative* performance revealing major classifications, categories, and contradictions of cultural processes." In these respects it might conceivably fulfill Huxley's fourth function, that of "serving as sexual or social bonding mechanisms," by transforming social and personal life-crises (birth, initiation, marriage, death) into occasions where symbols and values representing the unity and continuity of the total group were celebrated and reanimated. The cultural rituals which seem most to embody something resembling Huxley's definition of "ritualization" are "seasonal, agricultural, fertility, funerary, and healing ones, because they make explicit the interdependence of people with their physical environments and bodies."[5] But as I have written elsewhere, ritual is not necessarily a bastion of social conservatism; its symbols do not merely condense cherished sociocultural values. Rather, through its liminal processes, it holds the generating source of culture and structure. Hence, by definition ritual is associated with social *transitions* while *ceremony* is linked to social *states*. Performances of ritual are distinctive phases in the social process, whereby groups and individuals adjust to internal changes and adapt to their external environment.

Meyer Fortes, William Wyse Professor of Anthropology and Archaeology at Cambridge, influenced by Sigmund Freud, defined ritual at the London conference as "procedure for prehending the occult, that is, first, for grasping what is, for a particular culture, occult (i.e., beyond everyday human understanding, hidden, mysterious) in the events and incidents of people's lives, secondly, for binding what is so grasped by means of the ritual resources and beliefs available in that culture, and thirdly for thus incorporating what is grasped and bound into the normal existence of individuals and groups."[6] This formulation might well identify psychoanalytical clinical procedure as ritual process. Fortes makes his Freudian affiliation quite clear when he goes on to write that "ritual is concerned with prehending the unconscious (in the psychoanalytical sense) forces of individual action and existence, and their social equivalents, the irreducible factors in social relations (e.g. the mother-child nexus, at one end of the scale, the authority of society at the other). By bringing them, *suitably disguised,* or symbolized in tangible material objects and actions, into the open of social life, ritual binds them and makes them manageable" (italics added).[7]

Unlike Leach, Fortes sees ritual more as the handling of otherwise unmanageable power than the communication of important cultural knowledge. For Fortes irreducible ambiguities and antinomies are made visible and thus accessible to public and legitimate control—a position to which with important modifications I myself have subscribed—while for Leach the emphasis in ritual is cognitive and classificatory. As he writes, "it is characteristic of many ritual and mythical sequences in primitive society that the actors claim to be recapitulating the creation of the world and that this act of creation is mythologized as a list of names attached to persons, places, animals, and things. The world is created by the process of classification and the repetition of classification of itself perpetuates the knowledge which it incorporates."[8] Ritual's multicoded redundancies inscribe its "messages" on the minds of the participants. Clearly, the main difference between anthropologists of the Leachian persuasion and the ethologists in their concept of ritualization or ritual lay in the emphasis of the former on ritual as learned, culturally transmitted behavior, intrinsically linked with the development of language, and of the latter on ritual as genetically programmed behavior with important nonverbal components.

The Neurobiology of the Brain: Culturetype and Genotype

The years passed. I continued to treat ritual essentially as a cultural system. Meanwhile exciting new findings were coming from genetics, ethology, and neurology, particularly the neurobiology of the brain. I found myself asking a stream of questions more or less along the following lines. Can we enlarge our understanding of the ritual process by relating it to some of these findings? After all, can we escape from something like animal ritualization without escaping our own bodies and psyches, the rhythms and structures of which arise on their own? As Ronald Grimes has said, "They flow with or without our conscious assent; they are uttered-exclamations of nature and our bodies." [9] I also asked myself many of the questions raised by Ralph Wendell Burhoe[10] —especially, following Edward O. Wilson, what is the nature of the alleged "chain," and how long is it, by which genes hold cultural patterns, including ritual patterns, to use the idiom of sociobiology, "on leash"? This, it seemed to me, is where the neurobiology of the human brain begins to be relevant.

We shall have occasion to look at the findings of Paul MacLean, the neuroanatomist, again later, but something should be said now about his work on what might be called "archaic" structures of the human brain. His early work dealt with what is called the limbic system, an evolutionarily ancient part of the brain concerned with the emotions, cradled in or near the fringes of the cortex. In a 1949 paper he suggested that the limbic system is "the major circuit that would have to be involved in psychosomatic diseases, such as gastrointestinal ulcers caused by social or psychological stress, a now widely accepted hypothesis since it has been demonstrated that this system controls the pituitary gland at the base of the brain and the autonomic nervous systems, which in turn control the viscera." [11] He further proposed in 1952 that the frontal lobes of the cerebral hemispheres, shown to be "the seat of the highest human faculties, such as *foresight and concern for the consequences and meaning of events,* may have these functions and others *by virtue of intimate connections between the frontal lobes and the limbic system*" (italics added).[12] Here we see that the highest and newest portion of the cerebral cortex has by no means detached itself from an ancient "primitive" region, but functions as it does precisely "by virtue of its relationship to the old emotional circuitry."[13] Later, Walle Nauta, a celebrated neuroanatomist, has referred to the frontal lobes as "the neocortex of the limbic system."[14] As Melvin Konner concludes: "Just as other parts of the cortex have been identified as the highest report-and-control centers for vision, hearing, tactile sensation, and movement, so the frontal lobes have emerged as the highest report-and-control center for the emotions."[15] Thus evolutionarily recent and archaic patterns of innervation interarticulate, and the former is pliant to conditioning while the latter is quite resistant.

Paul MacLean's work, and related studies by Jason Brown, raised the question neatly formed by Burhoe: What is the role of the brain as an organ for the appropriate mixing of genetic and cultural information in the production of mental, verbal, or organic behavior? Burhoe raises further important questions: To what extent is the lower brain, including the limbic system and its behavior (to continue the metaphor), "on a very short leash" under the control of the genotype? (Konner uses the term genetically "hard wired.") In other words is genetic inheritance a definitive influence here? The corollary would seem to run as follows: To what extent is the upper brain, especially the neocortex, which is the area responsible in mammals for coordination and for higher mental abilities, on a longer leash in terms of control by the genotype or genome, the fundamental constitution of the organism in terms of its hereditary factors? Does socioculturally transmitted information *take over* control in humankind and, if so, what are the limits, if any, to its control? Does the genotype take a permanent back seat, and is social conditioning now all in all? The picture thus built up for me was a kind of *dual control* leading to what Burhoe calls a series of symbiotic coadaptations between what might be called culturetypes and genotypes. MacLean's hypothesis about the anatomical relations of the frontal lobes to the limbic system is certainly suggestive here. Subsequently MacLean went further and gave us his model of the "triune brain." (As we shall see later, J. P. Henry and P. M. Stephens have recently argued that the dominant or left cerebral hemisphere represents a fourth and phylogenetically most recent system peculiar to our species.)[16] According to his model, MacLean sees us as possessing three brains in one, rather than conceiving of the brain as a unity. Each has a different phylogenetic history, each has its own distinctive organization and make-up, although they are interlinked by millions of interconnections, and each has its own special intelligence, its own sense of time and space, and its own motor functions.[17] MacLean postulates that the brain evolved in three stages, producing parts of the brain which are still actively with us though modified and intercommunicating.

The first to evolve is the *reptilian brain.* This is the *brain stem,* an upward growth of the spinal cord and the most primitive part of the brain, which we share with all vertebrate creatures and which has remained remarkably unchanged throughout the myriads of years of evolution. In lizards and birds this brain is the dominant and controlling circuitry. It contains nuclei which control processes vital to the sustenance of life (i.e. the cardiovascular and respiratory systems). Whereas we can continue to exist without large portions of our cerebral hemispheres, without our reptilian brain we would be dead! What MacLean did was to show that this "structure" or "level," as some term the reptilian brain, whether in reptiles, birds, or mammals, is not only concerned with control of movement, but also with the storage and control of what is called "instinctive behavior"—the fixed action patterns and innate releasing mechanisms so often written about by the ethologists, the genetically preprogrammed perceptual-motor sequences such as emotional displays, territorial defense-behaviors, and nest-building. According to Brown, reptilian consciousness at the sensory-motor level is centered on the body itself and not differentiated from external space; yet it constitutes, I suppose, a preliminary form of consciousness. The reptilian brain also has nuclei which control the reticular activating system, which is responsible for alertness and the maintenance of consciousness. It is a regulator or integrator of behavior, a kind of traffic control center for the brain. Reptiles and birds, in which the *corpus striatum* seems to be the most highly developed part of the brain, have behavioral repertoires consisting of stereotyped behaviors and responses: a lizard turning sideways and displaying its dewlap as a threat, or a bird repeating again and again the same territorial song. I am not suggesting that mammals have no such behavior—clearly many have much—but rather that birds and reptiles have little else.

MacLean's "second brain" is the one he calls the *palaeomammalian* or "old mammalian brain." This seems to have arisen with the evolution of the earliest mammals, the monotremata, marsupials, and simpler placentals such as rodents. It is made up of those subcortical structures known as the midbrain, the most important components of which are the limbic system, including the hypothalamus (which contains centers controlling homeostatic mechanisms associated with heat, thirst, satiety, sex, pain and pleasure, and emotions of rage and fear), and the pituitary gland (which controls and integrates the activities of all the endocrine glands in the body). The old mammalian brain differs from the reptilian brain generally in that it is, as the neuroanatomist James Papez defines it, "*the stream of feeling*," while the older "level" is the "*stream of movement*." The hypothalamic and pituitary systems are homeostatic mechanisms *par excellence*; they maintain normal, internal stability in an organism by coordinating the responses of the organ systems that compensate for environmental changes. Later, we shall refer to such equilibrium-maintaining systems as "trophotropic," literally "responding to the 'nourishing (*trophē*) maintenance of organic systems," "keeping them going," as opposed to the "ergotropic" or aroused state of certain systems when they do "work" (*ergon*), "put themselves out," so to speak. The trophotropic systems, in Stevens' words,

> not only maintain a critical and supremely sensitive control of the hormone levels [hormones, of course, being substances formed in some organ of the body, usually a gland, and carried by a body fluid to another organ or tissue, where it has a specific effect] but also balance hunger against satiation, sexual desire against gratification, thirst against fluid retention, sleep against wakefulness. By this evolutionary stage, the primitive mammalian, the major emotions, fear and anger, have emerged, together with their associated behavioral responses of flight or fight. Conscious awareness is more in evidence and behavior is less rigidly determined by instincts, though these are still very much apparent. The areas concerned with these emotions and behaviors lie in the limbic system, which includes the oldest and most primitive part of the newly evolving cerebral cortex —the so-called *palaeocortex*. . . . In all mammals, including man, the midbrain is a structure of the utmost complexity, controlling the psychophysical economy and many basic responses and attitudes to the environment. An animal deprived of its cerebral cortex can still find its way about, feed itself, slake its thirst, and avoid painful stimuli, but it has difficulty in attributing function or "meaning" to things: a natural predator will be noticed, for example, but not apparently perceived as a threat. Thus, accurate perception and the attribution of meaning evidently requires the presence of the cerebral hemispheres.[18]

The *neo-mammalian* or "new mammalian" brain, the third in MacLean's model, corresponds to "the stream of thought" proposed by Papez and achieves its culmination in the complex mental functions of the human brain. Structurally, it is the *neocortex*—the outer layer of brain tissue or that part of the cerebrum which is rich in nerve-cell bodies and synapses. Some estimate there to be 10,000 million cells (10^{10}). Functionally, it is responsible for cognition and sophisticated perceptual processes as opposed to instinctive and affective behavior.

Further questions are triggered by MacLean's model of the triune brain. For example, how does it fit with Freud's model of the id, ego, and superego, with Carl Jung's model of the collective unconscious and archetypes, with neo-Darwinian theories of selection, and especially with cross-cultural anthropological studies and historical studies in comparative religion? One might further ask with Burhoe: To what extent is it true that human feelings, hopes, and fears of what is most sacred are a necessary ingredient in generating decisions and motivating their implementation? This question is connected with the problem of whether it is true that such information is necessarily filtered through the highly genetically programmed areas in the lower brain, the brain stem, and the limbic systems. Further questions now arise. For example, if ritualization, as discussed by Huxley, Lorenz, and other ethologists, has a biogenetic foundation, while meaning has a neocortical learned base, does this mean that creative processes, those which generate new cultural knowledge, might result from a coadaptation, perhaps in the ritual process itself, of genetic and cultural information? We also can ask whether the neocortex is the seat of programs largely structured by the culture through the transmission of linguistic and other symbol systems to modify the expression of genetic programs. How far, we might add, do these higher symbols, including those of religion and ritual, derive their meaning and force for action from their association with earlier established neural levels of animal ritualization? I will discuss this later in connection wtih my field data on Central African ritual symbols.

Hemispheric Lateralization

Before I examine some recent conjectures about the consequences for the study of religion of a possible coadaptation of cultures and gene pools, I should say something about the "lateralization" (the division into left and right) of the cerebral hemispheres and the division of control functions between the left and right hemispheres. The work of the surgeons P. Vogel, J. Bogen, and their associates at the California Institute of Technology in the early sixties, in surgically separating the left hemisphere from the right hemisphere to control epilepsy by cutting the connections between the two, particularly the inch-long, quarter-inch thick bundle of fibers called the *corpus callosum,* led to the devising of a number of techniques by R. W. Sperry (who won a Nobel Prize in 1981), Michael Gazzaniga, and others which gained unambiguous evidence about the roles assumed by each hemisphere in their patients. In 1979, an important book appeared, *The Spectrum of Ritual,* edited and partly authored by Eugene d'Aquili, Charles D. Laughlin, and John McManus.[19] In an excellent overview of the literature on ritual trance from the neurophysiological perspective, Barbara Lex summarizes the findings of current research on hemispheric lateralization. She writes: "In most human beings, the left cerebral hemisphere functions in the production of speech, as well as in linear, analytic thought, and also assesses the duration of temporal units, processing information sequentially. In contrast, the specializations of the right hemisphere comprise spatial and tonal perception, recognition of patterns–including those constituting emotion and other states in the internal milieu–and holistic, synthetic thought, but its linguistic capability is limited and the temporal capacity is believed absent. Specific acts involved complementary shifts between the functions of the two hemispheres.[20] Howard Gardner, following Gazzaniga, suggests that

> at birth we are all split-brained individuals. This may be literally true, since the corpus callosum which connects the hemispheres appears to be nonfunctional at birth. Thus, in early life, each hemisphere appears to participate in all of learning. It is only when, for some unknown reason, the left side of the brain takes the lead in manipulating objects, and the child begins to speak, that the first signs of asymmetry are discernible. At this time the corpus callosum is gradually beginning to function. For a number of years, learning of diverse sorts appears to occur in both hemispheres, but there is a gradual shift of dominant motor functions to the left hemisphere, while visual-spatial functions are presumably migrating to the right. . . . The division of labor grows increasingly marked, until, in the post-adolescent period, each hemisphere becomes incapable of executing the activities that the other hemisphere dominates, either because it no longer has access to its early learning, or because early traces have begun to atrophy through disuse.[21]

D'Aquili and Laughlin hold that both hemispheres operate in solving problems "via a mechanism of mutual inhibition controlled at the brain stem level." The world "is approached by a rapid functional alternation of each hemisphere. One is, as it were, flashed on, then turned off; the second flashed on, then turned off. The rhythm of this process and the predominance of one side or the other may account for various cognitive styles [one thinks of Pascal's contrast between *'l'esprit de geometrie'* and *'l'esprit de finesse'*], from the extremely analytic and scientific to the extremely artistic and synthetic."[22] These authors and Lex then make an interesting attempt to link the dual functioning of the hemispheres with W. R. Hess's model of the dual functioning of what are termed the ergotropic and trophotropic systems within the central nervous system, as a way of exploring and explaining phenomena reported in the study of ritual behavior and meditative states.[23] Let me explain these terms. As its derivation from the Greek *ergon* ("work") suggests, ergotropic is related to any energy-expending process within the nervous system. It consists not only of the sympathetic nervous system, which governs arousal states and fight or flight responses, but also such processes as increased heart rate, blood pressure, sweat secretion as well as increased secretion of catabolic hormones, epinephrine (a hormone secreted by the medulla of the adrenal gland, which stimulates the heart and increases muscular strength and endurance) and other stimulators. Generally speaking, the ergotropic system affects behavior in the direction of arousal, heightened activity, and emotional responsiveness, suggesting such colloquialisms as "warming up" and "getting high." The trophotropic system (*trophē*, in Greek, means nourishment –here the idea is of system-sustaining) includes not only the parasympathetic nervous system, which governs basic vegetative and homeostatic functions, but also any central nervous system process that maintains the baseline stability of the organism, for example, reduction in heart rate, blood pressure, sweat secretion, pupillary constriction as well as increased secretion of insulin, estrogens, androgens, and so on. Briefly, the trophotropic system makes for inactivity, drowsiness, sleep, "cooling down," and trance-like states.[24]

Developing the work of Hess, d'Aquili and Laughlin propose an extended model, "according to which the minor or nondominant hemisphere [usually the right hemisphere] is identified with the trophotropic or baseline energy state system, and the dominant or major hemisphere [usually the left] that governs analytical verbal and causal thinking is identified with the ergotropic or energy-expending system."[25] They present evidence which suggests that when either the ergotropic or trophotropic system is hyperstimulated, there results a "spillover" into the opposite system after "three stages of tuning," often by "driving behaviors" employed to facilitate ritual trance. They also use the term "rebound" from one system to the other; they find that when the left hemisphere is stimulated beyond a certain threshold, the right hemisphere is also stimulated. In particular, they postulate that the rhythmic activity of ritual, aided by sonic, visual, photic, and other kinds of "driving," may lead in time to simultaneous maximal stimulation of both systems, causing ritual participants to experience what the authors call "positive, ineffable affect." They also use Freud's term "oceanic experience," as well as "yogic ecstasy," also the Christian term *unio mystica,* an experience of the union of those cognitively discriminated opposites, typically generated by binary, digital left-hemispherical ratiocination. I suppose one might also use the Zen term *satori* (the integrating flash), and one could add the Quakers' "inner light," Thomas Merton's "transcendental consciousness," and the yogic *samadhi.*[26]

D'Aquili and Laughlin believe that though the end point of the simultaneous strong discharge of both the ergotropic and trophotropic systems is the same in meditation and ritual, the former begins by intensely stimulating the trophotropic system through techniques for reducing thought and desire in order to maintain "an almost total baseline homeostasis."[27] This results in "spillover" to the ergotropic side, and eventually to strong excitation of both systems. Ritual, on the other hand, involves initial ergotrophic excitation. The authors have previously speculated that *causal* thinking arises from the reciprocal interconnections of the inferior parietal lobule and the anterior convexity of the frontal lobes, particularly on the dominant, usually left side, and is an inescapable human propensity. They call this brain nexus "the causal operator" and claim that it "grinds out the initial terminus or first cause of any strip of reality."[28] They argue that "gods, powers, spirits, personified forces, or any other causative ingredients are automatically generated by the causal operator."[29] Untoward events particularly cry out for a cause. Hence "human beings have *no choice* but to construct myths to explain their world," to orient themselves "in what often appears to be a capricious universe." Cause-seeking is "inherent in the obligatory functioning of the neural structures." We are, indeed, back, via neurobiology it would seem, to Aristotle's "first cause that is uncaused" or "Prime Mover unmoved"! We humans cannot do otherwise than postulate first causes to explain what we observe. They write, "since it is highly unlikely that humankind will ever know the first cause of every strip of reality observed, it is highly probable that humankind will always create gods, powers, demons, or other entities as first causes."[30]

Myths present problems to the verbal analytic consciousness. Claude Lévi-Strauss has made us familiar with some of these problems: life and death, good and evil, mutability and an unchangeable "ground of being," the one and the many, freedom and necessity, and a few other perennial "posers."[31] Myths attempt to explain away such logical contradictions, but puzzlement remains at the cognitive left-hemispherical level. D'Aquili and Laughlin argue that *ritual* is often performed situationally to resolve problems posed by myth to the analytic verbalizing consciousness. This is because like all other animals, man attempts to master the environmental situation by means of motor behavior, in this case ritual, a mode going back into his phylogenetic past and involving repetitive motor, visual, and auditory driving stimuli, kinetic rhythms, repeated prayers, mantras, and chanting, which strongly activate the ergotropic system.[32] Ergotropic excitation is appropriate because the problem is presented in the "mythical" analytical mode, which involves binary thinking, mediations, and causal chains arranging both concepts and percepts in terms of antinomies or polar dyads. These are mainly left-hemispheric properties and connect up, in the authors' view, with the augmented sympathetic discharges mentioned earlier: increased heart rate, blood pressure, sweat secretion, pupillary dilation, increased secretion of catabolic hormones, and so on. If excitation continues long enough the trophotropic system is triggered too, with mixed discharges from both sides, resulting often in ritual trance. Lex writes that "driving techniques [also] facilitate right-hemisphere dominance, resulting in gestalt, timeless, nonverbal experiences, differentiated and unique when compared with left-hemisphere functioning or hemisphere alternation."[33] One solution, if it can be so termed, of the Sphinxian riddles posed by myth, according to d'Aquili and Laughlin, is that "during certain ritual and meditation states, logical paradoxes or the awareness of polar opposites as presented in myth appear simultaneously, *both* as antinomies and as unified wholes" (italics added).[34] There is an ecstatic state and a sense of union, brief in ritual, prolonged in meditation, where culturally transmitted techniques and intense personal discipline sustain the peak experience. One is aware of paradox, but rejoices in it, reminding one of Sören Kierkegaard's joyous celebration of the paradox of the cross as the heart of Christianity.

The problem therefore is resolved in d'Aquili and Laughlin's view not at the cognitive, left-hemispheric level but directly by an experience which is described by the authors as ineffable, that is, literally beyond verbal expression. Presumably the frequent embodiment or embedment of the myth in the ritual scenario, either verbally in prayer or song, or nonverbally in dramatic action or visual symbolism, continues to arouse within the ritual context the "cognitive ergotropic functions of the dominant hemisphere."[35] If the experiences of participants have been rewarding—and ritual devices and symbolic actions may well tune a wide range of individuals (amounting to the well-known redundancy of ritual with its many sensory codes and multivocal symbols)—faith in the cosmic and moral orders contained in the myth cycle will obviously be reinforced. A. J. Mandell argues in "Towards a Psychobiology of Transcendence" that "transcendent consciousness, suggested by William James to be the primary religious experience, is a neurochemically and neurophysiologically definable state, an imperturbable hypomania . . . blissful, empathic, and creative."[36]

Play

It is clear that all this refers to the serious work of the brain, as distinct from "play." Full ergotropic, left-hemisphere behavior tends to be dramatic, agonistic behavior. I am not too happy about some authors' tendency to localize mental functions somewhat specifically in cortical regions rather than in interrelational networks, but there does seem to be, broadly speaking, something in the division of labor between the hemispheres, in the different work they do. The term "ergotropic," as we have seen, is derived from the Greek *ergon*, "work" and *tropos* "a turn, way, manner." It represents the autonomic nervous system in the mode of work, as a sympathetic subsystem, whereas the trophotropic system (from the Greek *trophē*, "food, nourishment") represents the autonomic nervous system in the mode of sustentation, as a parasympathetic subsystem responsible for producing a balance of functions and of chemical composition within an organism. This too is a kind of diffused work, less focused and mobilized, less intense than the ergotropic functions. But where does "play" play a part in this model? One seldom sees much mention of play in connection with brain neurophysiology. Yet play is a kind of dialectical dancing partner of ritual, and ethologists give play behavior equal weight with ritualization. D'Aquili and Laughlin hardly mention the word.

The hemispheres clearly have their *work* to do, and the autonomic nervous system has its *work* to do. The one makes for social dramas, the other for social routines. Whether normally functioning or intensely stimulated, the components of the central nervous system seem to have clearly assigned, responsible, interdependent roles to perform. One might speculate that at the neurobiological level play might have something to do with the sensitization of the neural structures of an interface type, like the limbic system at the core of the brain, which is known to be intimately associated with the expression of emotion, particularly with the experience of pleasure, pain, and anger. We will return to this later.

As I see it, play does not fit in anywhere particular; it is a transient and is recalcitrant to localization, to placement, to fixation—a joker in the neuroanthropological act. Johann Huizinga, and Karl Groos before him, dubbed it a free activity, but Huizinga, Roger Caillois, and many afterwards have commented on the enclosure of playing with frames of "arbitrary, imperative, and purposely tedious conventions."[37] Playfulness is a volatile, sometimes dangerously explosive essence, which cultural institutions seek to bottle or contain in the vials of games of competition, chance, and strength, in modes of simulation such as theater, and in controlled disorientation, from roller coasters to dervish dancing—Caillois' "ilinx" or vertigo. Play could be termed dangerous because it may subvert the left-right hemispheric regular switching involved in maintaining social order. Most definitions of play involve notions of disengagement, of free-wheeling, of being out of mesh with the serious, "bread-and-butter," let alone "life-and-death" processes of production, social control, "getting and spending," and raising the next generation. The neuronic energies of play, as it were, lightly skim over the cerebral cortices, sampling rather than partaking of the capacities and functions of the various areas of the brain. As Don Handelman and Gregory Bateson have written that is possibly why play can provide a metalanguage (since to be "meta" is to be both beyond and between) and emit metamessages about so many and varied human propensities, and thus provide, as Handelman has said, "a very wide *range* of commentary on the social order."[38] Play can be everywhere and nowhere, imitate anything, yet be identified with nothing. Play is "transcendent" (to use Edward Norbeck's term), though only just so, brushing the surfaces of more specialized neural organizations rather than existing apart from them or looking down from a godlike height on them. Play is the supreme *bricoleur* of frail transient constructions, like a caddis worm's case or a magpie's nest in nature. Its metamessages are composed of a potpourri of apparently incongruous elements: products of both hemispheres are juxtaposed and intermingled. Passages of seemingly wholly rational thought jostle in a Joycean or surrealist manner with passages filleted of all syntactical connectedness. Yet, although "spinning loose" as it were, the wheel of play reveals to us (as Mihaly Csikszentmihalyi has argued)[39] the possibility of changing our goals and, therefore, the restructuring of what our culture states to be reality.

You may have guessed that play is, for me, a liminal or liminoid mode, essentially interstitial, betwixt-and-between all standard taxonomic nodes, essentially "elusive"—a term derived from the Latin *ex* for "away" plus *ludere,* "to play"; hence the Latin verb *eludere* acquired the sense of "to take away from someone at play," thus "to cheat" or "to deceive." As such play cannot be pinned down by formulations of left-hemisphere thinking—such as we all must use in keeping with the rhetorical conventions of academic discourse. Play is neither ritual action nor meditation, nor is it merely vegetative, nor is it just "having fun"; it also has a good deal of ergotropic and agonistic aggressivity in its odd-jobbing, *bricolage* style. As Roger Abrahams has remarked, it makes fun of people, things, ideas, ideologies, institutions, and structures; it is partly a mocker as well as a mimic and a tease, arousing hope, desire, or curiosity without always giving satisfaction.[40] It is as much a reflexive interrupter as an inciter of what Csikszentmihalyi has described as flow states. Like many Trickster figures in myths (or should these be "antimyths," if myths are dominantly left-hemisphere speculations about causality?) play can deceive, betray, beguile, delude (another derivation of *ludere* "to play"), dupe, hoodwink, bamboozle, and gull—as that category of players known as "cardsharps" well know! Actually, Walter Skeat derives the English verb "play" itself from the Anglo-Saxon *plegian,* "to strike or clap"; the Anglo-Saxon noun *plega* means not only "a game, sport," but also, commonly, "a fight, battle" (here again with ergotropic implications).

Play, as stated earlier, draws its materials from all aspects of experience, both from the interior milieu and the external environment. Yet, as Handelman writes, it has no instrumental potency; it is, we might put it, a "shadow warrior," or *Kagemusha.*[41] For this very reason, its range of metacommunication is great; nothing human escapes it. Still, in its own oxymoronic style it has a dangerous harmlessness, for it has no fear. Its lightness and fleetingness protect it. It has the powers of the weak, an infantine audacity in the face of the strong. To ban play is, in fact, to massacre the innocents. If man is a neotenic species, play is perhaps his most appropriate mode of performance.

More than that, it is clear, as Konner points out, play is educative. The most intelligent and long-lived mammals have developed it most fully—the primates, the cetacea, and the terrestrial and aquatic carnivores. "It serves the functions of exercise, of learning about the environment and conspecifics, and in some species, of sharpening or even acquiring fundamental subsistence and social skills." Opportunity for observation of a task in the frame of "play" while or before trying to do it has been "shown to improve the rate of learning it in a number of mammals in experimental settings."[42] Play, then, is probably related to the higher cerebral centers—not forgetting its connection also with arousal and pleasure—particularly in rough and tumble games, where the limbic system is clearly engaged.

Yet serious violence is usually controlled objectively and culturally by rules and subjectively by inhibitory mechanisms of perhaps a different type from the Freudian superego or ego-defense mechanisms, although perhaps play does defend consciousness from some of the more dangerous unconscious drives.

Finally, play, like other liminal phenomena, is in the subjunctive mood. What does this mean? The subjunctive designates a verb form or set of forms used in English to express a contingent or hypothetical action. A contingent action is one that may occur but that is not likely or intended. Subjunctivity is possibility. It refers to what may or might be. It is also concerned with supposition, conjecture, and assumption, with the domain of "as-if" rather than "as-is." (Hence, there must be a good deal of left-hemispheric activity in play, linguistic and conceptual activity, but done for its own sweet sake.) "As-is" refers to the world of what culture recognizes as factuality, the world of cause and effect, expressed in the "indicative mood"—which indicated that the denoted act or condition is an objective fact. This is *par excellence* the world of the left cerebral hemisphere. The world of the right hemisphere is nevertheless, not identical with the world of play either, for its gestalt grasp of things holds for it the sense of a higher reality, beyond speculation or supposition. Play is a light-winged, light-fingered sceptic, a Puck between the day world of Theseus and the night world of Oberon, putting into question the cherished assumptions of both hemispheres, both worlds. There is no sanctity in play; it is irreverent and is protected in the world of power struggles by its apparent irrelevance and clown's garb. It is almost as though the limbic system were itself endowed with higher intelligence, in a kind of carnivalesque reversal of the indicative situation.

However, since play deals with the whole gamut of experience both contemporary and stored in culture, it can be said perhaps to play a similar role in the social construction of reality as mutation and variation in organic evolution. Its flickering knowledge of all experience possible to the nervous system and its detachment from that system's localizations enables it to perform the liminal function of ludic recombination of familiar elements in unfamiliar and often quite arbitrary patterns. Yet it may happen that a light, play-begotten pattern for living or social structuring, once thought whimsical, under conditions of extreme social change may prove an adaptive, "indicative mood" design for living. Here early theories that play arises from excess energy have renewed relevance. Part of that surplus fabricates ludic critiques of presentness, of the status quo, undermining it by parody, satire, irony, slapstick; part of it subverts past legitimacies and structures; part of it is mortgaged to the future in the form of a store of possible cultural and social structures, ranging from the bizarre and ludicrous to the utopian and idealistic, one of which may root in a future reality, allowing the serious dialectic of left- and right-hemispherical functions to propel individuals and groups of individuals from earth to heaven and heaven to earth within a new indicative mood frame. But it was the slippery Trickster who enabled them to do it, and he/she modestly, in Jacques Derrida's ludic words, "erases the trace."

The experiments of James Olds and Peter Milner, at the California Institute of Technology from 1953 onwards, on stimulating by implanted electrodes the hypothalamus of the brains of rats, including the parts radiating from the hypothalamus like spokes (neural pathways to the olfactory and limbic systems, the septal areas, amygdala, etc.), seem to have a bearing on the pleasures of play, but I have not followed up this avenue of enquiry.[43]

Further Questions on the Brain: Religion, Archetypes, and Dreaming

By indirections we seek out directions. This long digression on hemispherical lateralization, play, and cultural subjunctivity brings me back to some of Burhoe's questions that have been vexing me. One is: How does this picture of brain functioning and of the central nervous system accord with distinctive features of the varied religious systems that have survived to this point in time and exerted paradigmatic influence on major societies and cultures? Here we could profitably compare Eastern and Western religions and their variations. Can some be described as emphasizing in their cosmologies, theologies, rituals, meditative techniques, pilgrimages, and so on, right-hemispherical properties or left-hemispherical dominance? Do some emphasize rituals while others stress modes of meditation and contemplation as their central processes of worship? Again how does this picture fit with descriptions of the varieties of religious experience that have been noted by William James and his successors? Would it be a fruitful enterprise to foster experimental work on the varied genetic and experiential structurings of human brains which might throw light on aspects of religious experience and motivation? We will take a brief look later in this essay at some interesting guesswork by Jungians in relation to this problem. Conversely, can we illuminate, through cross-cultural comparison, the capacity of culturally shaped systems of rituals, symbols, myths, and rational structures to produce viable types of religious experience in the genetically varied population of brains? Here much more detailed descriptive work in the study of different kinds of ritual in a single religious system, as well as cross cultural and transhistorical studies of ritual systems, is imperative. So many questions: so few answers. But we can only do fruitful research if we first ask the right questions.

Naturally, the findings of neurophysiologists have provoked many speculations from members of other disciplines not directly concerned with the brain and its workings. The notion of the triune brain propounded by MacLean, for instance, has encouraged Jungian psychologists to claim that a neurological basis has been found for the collective unconscious and its archetypes. One Jungian, Anthony Stevens, has been impressed by the work of P. Flor-Henry and of G. E. Schwartz, R. J. Davidson, and F. Maer.[44] The latter showed that human emotional responses are dependent on neuronal pathways linking the limbic system of the midbrain (the old mammalian brain) with parietal and frontal areas of the right hemisphere. Flor-Henry found that this whole complicated right-hemispheric/limbic affectional system is under the surveillance and control of the left, I repeat, of the *left* frontal cortex. This lends additional testimony to the view that the left hemisphere (via the corpus callosum or the large cable of nerve fibers which connect the two cerebral hemispheres, functioning to transmit information between hemispheres and to coordinate their activities) can repress or inhibit the activities, especially the emotionally toned activities (which are the vital concern of psychiatrists), of the right. In my discussion of the possible neuronal base of play, you will recall, I guessed at a connection between the midbrain and human upper brain. If Flor-Henry is correct in supposing a left-hemisphere inhibiting effect, might not the propensity to play result from a temporary relaxation of the inhibitory effect, perhaps through the focused cultural means of framing and arousal?

All this leads Stevens to speculate rather interestingly about the relationship of various psychical processes recognized by depth psychology to what is known about the neurophysiology of the brain. His views also bear on the questions I have been raising about the possible nature of religion as at once a supergenetic and a superindividual agency developed from the coadaptation or integration of two semiautonomous systems. These are, in Burhoe's terms, first, basic genetic information and its biological expression, particularly in the lower levels of the brain, whose genetic programs are not so very different from those in protohuman hominids, and second, the specifically human generation of a living sociocultural system where the learning powers of the upper brain radically modify the common human gene pool, resulting in enormous cultural and phenotypical variation, that is, variation in manifest characteristics. Stevens argues, "While it may well be that psychic processes belonging to the personal 'Freudian' unconscious proceed in the right hemisphere, it seems probable that Jung was right when he guessed that the archetypal systems, if they could be given a local habitation and a name, must have their neuronal substrate located in the phylogenetically much older parts of the brain."[45]

For those who are unfamiliar with Jungian terminology, archetypes (according to Stevens' definition) are "innate neuropsychic centers possessing the capacity to initiate, control, and mediate the common behavioral characteristics and typical experiences of all human beings irrespective of cultural differences."[46] Jung himself, who rejected the view that humankind was a blank slate or a *tabula rasa* on which experience was prenatally[47] and postnatally inscribed, held that our species is born with numerous predispositions for perceiving, feeling, behaving, and conceptualizing in particular ways. As he put it:

> There is no human experience, nor would experience be possible at all without the intervention of a subjective aptitude. What is this subjective aptitude? Ultimately it consists of an innate psychic structure which allows man to have experiences of this kind. Thus the whole nature of the human male presupposes woman, both physically and spiritually. His system is tuned in to woman from the start, just as it is prepared for a quite definite world where there is water, light, air, salt, carbohydrates, etc. The form of the world into which he is born is already inborn in him as a virtual image. Likewise parents, wife,

> children, birth and death are inborn in him as virtual images, as psychic aptitudes. These *a priori* categories have by nature a collective character; they are images of parents, wife, and children in general, and are not individual predestinations [This is perhaps Jung's clearest formulation of what he means by archetypes.] We must therefore think of these images as lacking in solid content, hence as unconscious. They only acquire solidity, influence, and eventual consciousness in the encounter with empirical facts which touch the unconscious aptitude and quicken it to life. They are, in a sense, the deposits of all our ancestral experiences, but they are not the experiences themselves.[48]

Archetypes manifest themselves subjectively in such things as dreams, fantasies, writing, poetry, painting and objectively in such collective representations as myths, rituals, and cultural symbols—and in many other modalities. Jung speaks of the Family archetype, the Feminine archetype, the God archetype, the Hero archetype, the Mother archetype, the Masculine archetype, the Wise Old Man archetype, using capital letters to distinguish them from the identically named roles occupied by actual historical individuals.

Stevens thinks it is impossible to locate any of the archetypes in any precise neurological fashion. Each must have "an extremely complex and widely ramifying neurological substrate involving millions of neurons in the brain stem and limbic system (the instinctive or biological pole) and *both* cerebral hemispheres (the psychic or spiritual pole)."[49] However, E. Rossi, another Jungian psychologist, argues that it is the right hemisphere which principally processes archetypal components, since "Jung's concepts of archetype, collective unconscious, and symbol are more closely associated with the use of the imagery, gestalt, and visuospatial characteristics of right hemispheric functioning."[50] Rossi also insists that, although the archetype is an imprint or pattern—perhaps a "trace"—which exists independently of the unconscious ego, it constantly comes under left hemispheric processing in the form of words, concepts, and language. But when this happens the archetypes, he writes "take their color from the individual consciousness in which they happen to appear."[51] Thus they are, so to speak, superficially denatured and clothed in the vestments provided by individual memory and cultural conditioning.

It is because of the difficulty of translating right-hemispherical processes into the logical, verbal formulations of the left brain that some emissions into ego consciousness of archetypal images are perceived as numinous, awesome, and mysterious, or uncanny, preternaturally strange. They seem to be clad in primordial authority undetermined by anything known or learned. Henry and Stephens consider that both hemispheres are able to suppress communication from the limbic system.[52] We have seen how the left hemisphere may inhibit communication from the right. Henry and Stephens believe that psychic health and personality integration depend as much on the maintenance of open communication between limbic system and cortex as on interhemispheric communication. They suggest that the neurophysiological function of dreaming is to facilitate integration of processes occuring in the limbic system with those of the cerebral hemisphere. This would fit well with Jung's views as well as with the French sleep expert Michel Jouvet's findings that the low voltage, high frequency EEG waves characteristic of dreaming sleep originate in the brain stem and spread upward through the midbrain to the cortex—perhaps bringing information from various levels of the unconscious.[53] Perhaps dreams, like the ritual symbols I have analyzed, are laminated, accreting semantic layers, as they move from brain stem through limbic system to the right hemisphere before final processing or editing by left hemispheric processes.

The Composite Brain and the Bipolar Symbol

These findings are interesting when related to my fieldwork among the Ndembu, a matrilineal society of northwest Zambia, during the 1950s. I discovered that what I called dominant or pivotal symbols in their ritual processes were not only possessors of multiple meanings but also had the property of polarization. For example, a tree which exuded a milky white latex was the dominant symbol of the girls puberty ritual (the novice was laid under a consecrated "milk tree" wrapped in a blanket, where she had to lie motionless throughout the whole long day while initiated women danced around her and the tree). The whole milk tree site, almost *mise-en-scène* was called *ifwilu,* which means "place of dying," for it was there that she died from her childhood. At this point she was separated from her own mother, who took minimal part in the ritual. But the milk tree (*mudyi*) was intimately connected with motherhood. I pieced together its many meanings from talking to many informants during many performances at which my wife and I were present, and have written about this research in several books, including *The Forest of Symbols* and *The Drums of Affliction.*[54] Briefly, the milk tree was said to "be" (more than merely to "represent") mother's milk, lactation, breasts, and nubility, at what could be called the physiological or orectic pole of its meaning. "Orectic" is a term used by philosophers, and was formerly quite popular among psychologists meaning "of or characterized by appetite or desire."

But the milk tree also "was" the matrilineage of the girl novice; it was where "the ancestress slept, where they initiated her and another ancestress and then another down to the grandmother and the mother and ourselves the children. It is a place where our tribe (*muchids*) began —and also the men in just the same way."[55] Thus it was more than a particular matrilineage; it was the principle of matriliny itself. It was even the whole Ndembu nation, one of whose distinctive features was its matrilineal organization. At some episodes of the long complex ritual, the milk tree was also said to stand for women and for womanhood. Another meaning, indexical rather than iconic, represented the milk tree as the relationship between the novice and her own mother in that place and at that time. It indicated that the relationship would be transformed by the performative action, since the daughter was no longer a dependent child but would become, like her mother, a married woman after the ritual seclusion and the coming-out rites were over and was potentially a mother herself. I called this more abstract set of meanings the normative or ideological pole, since it referred to principles of social organization, social categories, and values.

The milk tree also has other denotations and connotations, but it has struck me recently that these layers of meaning might well relate to what is being discovered about the functions of the brain. The orectic pole, referring to physical mothering and lactation, and charged with desire—the novice's desire to be fully a woman, the desire of the mature women to add a recruit to their number, the desire of a lineage for replenishment, the future bridegroom's desire for the novice (represented by the insertion of an arrow presented by the bridegroom into the ground among the roots of the milk tree) and many other modalities of desire—the orectic pole, then, surely has some connection with the functions of the limbic system, the old mammalian brain. This system MacLean calls the visceral brain because of its close connections to control centers for drive and emotion. Structures in the limbic system are believed to be the sites of action of many psychotropic drugs, including antipsychotic tranquilizers (e.g., Thorazine) and hallucinogens (e.g., LSD). In the ritual itself, with its powerful drumming and insurgent singing in which the women lampoon and deride the men, we observe ways of arousing the ergotropic system and the left-hemispheric functions of critical, linear thought. We can also see a triggering of the right-hemispheric apprehensions of pattern and holism by finally including the men in the ritual action and making them part of a scenario in which the novice is borne off to a newly made seclusion hut on the margin of the village, where she will undergo liminal instruction by female elders for many months, before "coming out" in a ritual which is also the precursor of her marriage.

Clearly, too, the normative pole of meaning including the references to matriliny, womanhood, tribal unity and continuity, and the mother-child bond, has connections with upper brain activities involving both hemispheres. One might speculate that the Jungian archetype of the Great Mother and the difficulty, resolved among the Ndembu by prolonged and sometimes painful initiation ritual, of separation from the archetypal power of the Great Mother is in some way connected with the milk tree symbolism and with the ritual behavior associated with it. It is interesting to me that a dominant symbol—every ritual system has several of them—should replicate in its structural and semantic make-up what are coming to be seen as key neurological features of the brain and central nervous system.

Conclusion

Does the new work on the brain further our species' self-understanding? Clearly an extreme ethological view of human society as rigidly genetically determined is as uninformative as an extreme behaviorist view of the human brain as a *tabula rasa* written on by experience. According to the extreme ecologists, we are "innately aggressive, acquisitive, nationalistic, capitalistic, and destructive."[56] Some of them announced our doom by overcrowding or urge the space race as a means of channeling aggressiveness. Some even give veiled approval to limited war or natural population control by drought, famine, or plague, as the means of securing ecological balance. While B. F. Skinner would modify and adapt us by environmental manipulation, reminding me irresistibly of H. G. Wells's *First Men on the Moon* in which the Selenites (the original Moonies), an insect species, were quite literally shaped by biological and psychological techniques to perform the labor appropriate to their caste, some ethologists would argue that our genetics damn us, despite our intelligence and will to survive. Ragnarok, not Walden II, will be the end of history. Hence the vogue for doom talk about such inevitabilities as ecocide, population explosion, and innate aggressiveness. Surely, a middle path is possible. Cannot we see those modalities of human perception and conceptualization, the lower brain and the upper brain, the archaic and recent systems of innervation as having been for at least several millions of years in active mutual confrontation?

It seems to me that religion may be partly the product of humanity's intuitions of its dual interiority and the fruitful creative Spirit generated by the interplay of the gene pool, as the Ancient of Days, and the upper brain, as Logos, to use the intuitive language of one historical religion, Christianity. The Filioque principle (the Spirit proceeding from the Father and the Son), Western Christians might say! Since culture is in one sense, to paraphrase Wilhelm Dilthey, objectivated and crystallized mentality (*Geist*), it may well be that some cultures reinforce one or another semiautonomous cerebral system at the expense of others through education and other modes of conditioning. This results in conflict between them or repression of one by another, instead of free interplay and mutual support—what is sometimes called love.

As you can see, I have been asking questions and making guesses in this paper rather than coming up with answers. My career focus mostly has been on the ritual process, a cultural phenomenon, more than on brain neuroanatomy and neurophysiology. But I am at least half convinced that there can be genuine dialogue between neurology and culturology, since both take into account the capacity of the upper brain for adaptability, resilience, learning, and symbolizing, in ways perhaps neglected by the ethologists *pur sang,* who seem to stop short in their thinking about ritualization at the more obviously genetically programmed behaviors of the lower brain. It is to the dialectic, and even contradiction at times, between the various semiautonomous systems of the developed and archaic structures of innervation, particularly those of the human brain, that we should look for the formulation of testable hypotheses about the ritual process and its role as performing noetic functions in ways peculiar to itself, as a *sui generis* mode of knowing.

Let me conclude by reassuring those who may have obtained the impression that all I am saying is that ritual is nothing but the structure and functioning of the brain writ large, or that I am reducing ritual to cerebral neurology, that I am really speaking of a global population of brains inhabiting an entire world of inanimate and animate entities, a population whose members are incessantly communicating with one another through every physical and mental instrumentality. But if one considers the geology, so to speak, of the human brain and nervous system, we see represented in its strata—each layer still vitally alive—not dead like stone, the numerous pasts and presents of our planet. Like Walt Whitman, we "embrace multitudes." And even our reptilian and palaeomammalian brains are human, linked in infinitely complex ways to the conditionable upper brain and kindling it with their powers. Each of us is a microcosm, related in the deepest ways to the whole life-history of that lovely deep blue globe swirled over with the white whorls first photographed by Edwin Aldrin and Neil Armstrong from their primitive space chariot, the work nevertheless of many collaborating human brains. The meaning of that living macrocosm may not only be found deep within us but also played from one mind to another as history goes on—with ever finer tuning—by the most sensitive and eloquent instrument of Gaea the Earth-spirit—the cerebral organ.

NOTES

1. Anthony Stevens, *Archetypes: A Natural History of the Self* (New York: Morrow, 1982), 24.

2. Robin Fox, *Encounter with Anthropology* (New York: Harcourt Brace Jovanovich, 1973), 13.

3. E. R. Leach, "Ritualization in Man in Relation to Conceptual and Social Development," in *A Discussion on Ritualization of Behaviors in Animals and Man,* ed. Julian Huxley, Philosophical Transactions of the Royal Society of London, series B. vol. 251, Biological Sciences (London, Royal Society, 1966), 403.

4. Julian Huxley, "Introduction," in *Discussion on Ritualization,* 250.

5. Ronald Grimes, *Beginnings in Ritual Studies* (Washington, D.C.: University Press of America, 1982), 34.

6. Meyer Fortes, "Religious Premisses and Logical Technique in Divinatory Ritual" in *Discussion of Ritualization,* 411.

7. Ibid., 413.

8. Leach, 405.

9. Grimes, 36.

10. See *Zygon,* vol. 18, no. 3 (September 1983) for Burhoe's questions.

11. Quoted in Melvin Konner, *The Tangled Wing: Biological Constraints on the Human Spirit* (New York: Holt Rinehart & Winston, 1982), 147.

12. Ibid.

13. Ibid.

14. Walle Nauta elaborated this outlook in "The Problem of the Frontal Lobe: A Reinterpretation," *Journal of Psychiatric Research* 8 (1971): 167-187.

15. Konner, 147.

16. J. P. Henry and P. M. Stephens, *Stress, Health, and the Social Environment* (New York: Springer-Verlag, 1977).

17. Paul D. MacLean, "Sensory and Perceptive Factors in Emotional Functions of the Triune Brain," in *Biological Foundations of*

Psychiatry, ed. R. G. Grenell and S. Gabay. 2 vols. (New York: Raven Press, 1976). 1:177–198. See also idem, "A Triune Concept of the Brain and Behavior," in *The Hincks Memorial Lectures,* ed. T. Boag and D. Campbell (Toronto: University of Toronto Press, 1973), 6–66; "On the Evolution of Three Mentalities," *Man-Environment Systems* 5 (1975): 213–224, reprinted in *New Dimensions in Psychiatry: A World View,* ed. S. Ariete and G. Chrzanowski, 2 vols. (New York: John Wiley & Sons, 1977), 2:305–328; and "Evolution of the Psychencephalon," *Zygon* 17 (June 1982): 187–211. Cf. J. Brown, *Mind, Brain, and Consciousness* (New York: Academic Press, 1977).

18. Stevens, 264–265.

19. Eugene G. d'Aquili et al., *The Spectrum of Ritual: A Biogenetic Structural Analysis* (New York: Columbia University Press, 1979).

20. Barbara Lex, "Neurobiology of Ritual Trance," in *Spectrum of Ritual,* 125.

21. Howard Gardner, *The Shattered Mind* (New York: Vintage, 1975), 386.

22. Eugene G. d'Aquili and Charles D. Laughlin, Jr., "The Neurobiology of Myth and Ritual," in *Spectrum of Ritual,* 174.

23. W. R. Hess, *On the Relationship Between Psychic and Vegetative Functions* (Zurich: Schwabe, 1925).

24. E. Gellhorn and W. F. Kiely, "Mystical States of Consciousness: Neurophysiological and Clinical Aspects," *Journal of Mental and Nervous Diseases* 154 (1972): 339–405.

25. D'Aquili and Laughlin, 175.

26. See Arnold J. Mandell, "Toward a Psychobiology of Transcendence," in *The Psychobiology of Consciousness,* ed. J. M. Davidson and J. R. Davidson (New York: Olenum, 1978), 80.

27. D'Aquili and Laughlin, 176.

28. Ibid., 170.

29. Ibid.

30. Ibid., 171.

31. C. Levi-Strauss, *Structural Anthropology* (New York: Anchor Books, 1963): idem, *The Savage Mind* (Chicago: University of Chicago Press, 1963); idem, *Mythologiques: Le cru et le cuit* (Paris: Plon, 1964).

32. D'Aquili and Laughlin, 177.

33. Lex, 146.

34. D'Aquili and Laughlin, 176.

35. Ibid., 177.

36. Mandell, 1.

37. Roger Caillois, *Man, Play, and Games* (New York: Schocken Books, 1979), 13.

38. Don Handelman, "Play and Ritual: Complementary Frames of Metacommunication," in *It's A Funny Thing, Humour,* ed. A. J. Chapman and H. Fort (London: Pergamon, 1977), 189.

39. Mihaly Csikszentmihalyi, *Beyond Boredom and Anxiety* (San Francisco: Jossey-Bass, 1975).

40. Roger Abrahams, personal communication both in a letter and in an essay.

41. See Akira Kurasawa's film, *Kagemusha.*

42. Konner, 246–247.

43. James Olds, "Behavioral Studies of Hypothalamic Functions," in *Biological Foundations of Psychiatry,* ed. R. Grenell and S. Gabay, vol. 1 (New York: Raven, 1976).

44. P. Flor-Henry, "Lateralized Temporal-Limbic Dysfunction and Psychopathology," *Annals of the New York Academy of Science* 380 (1976): 777–797; G. E. Schwartz, R. J. Davidson, and F. Maer, "Right Hemisphere Lateralization for Emotion in the Human Brain: Interaction with Cognition," *Science* 190 (1975): 286–288.

45. Stevens, 265–266.

46. Ibid., 296.

47. Experience begins in the womb, and child psychologists hold that communication between mother and child correlates with the development of neuronal pathways in the foetal brain. See for example Colwyn Trevarthen, "Cerebral Embryology and the Split Brain," in *Hemispheric Disconnection and Cerebral Function,* ed. M. Kinsbourne and W. L. Smith (Springfield, Illinois: Charles C. Thomas, 1974), 208–236.

48. Carl Jung, *Collected Works,* vol. 7, *Two Essays on Analytical Psychology* (Princeton: Princeton Unversity Press, 1972), paragraph 300.

49. Stevens, 266.

50. Cited in Stevens, 266.

51. Ibid.

52. Henry and Stephens, see note 16.

53. Michel Jouvet, "The Function of Dreaming: A Neurophysiologist's Point of View," in *Handbook of Psychology,* ed. M. S. Gazzaniga and C. Blakemore (New York: Academic Press, 1975).

54. Victor Turner, *The Forest of Symbols* (Ithaca, N.Y.: Cornell University Press, 1967); idem, *The Drums of Affliction* (Oxford: Clarendon Press, 1968).

55. Turner, *Drums of Affliction,* 198–268.

56. A point well made by Steven Rose, *The Conscious Brain* (New York: Vintage Books, 1976), 351.

Cultural Materialism: Alarums and Excursions

MARVIN HARRIS

Basic Principles

Cultural Materialism (C.M.) is a scientific research strategy for the development of an integrated corpus of causal theories about the evolution of differences and similarities in the global repertory of sociocultural systems. C.M.'s basic epistemological and theoretical principles can be set forth in six steps:

1. *Science as a distinct form of knowledge.* C.M.'s claim to scientific status rests on specific epistemological criteria which separate C.M. from humanist and aesthetic research strategies. Scientific knowledge is obtained by public, replicable operations (observations and logical transformations). The aim of science is to formulate explanatory theories which are predictive (or retrodictive), testable (or falsifiable), parsimonious, of broad scope, and integratable within a coherent corpus of other scientific theories. These criteria derive from the logical positivist and empiricist philosophical traditions as well as from the modern critique of that tradition by Popper (1965), Lakatos (1970), and Kuhn (1970; 1977).

The same criteria distinguish scientific theories which are more acceptable from those which are less acceptable. Scientific theories find acceptance in accordance with their relative powers of predictability, testability, parsimony, scope, and integratability as compared with rival theories about the same phenomena. Of course, since these criteria can only be fulfilled asymptotically, scientific theories are held as tentative approximations, never as unassailable dogmas.

2. *Behavior vs. Thought and Emics vs. Etics.* As a materialist research strategy, C.M. insists on the separation of descriptions of thought (or mental events) from behavior and on the separation of events viewed from the emic and etic perspectives. Behavioral events and mental events are not knowable through the same set of operations (observational procedures). Hence, in the tradition of empiricism, operationalism, and behaviorism, mental and behavioral events necessarily constitute separate domains of phenomena (whose relatedness is to be discovered, never assumed). Given the separation of these domains, there remains a second set of options that must be considered. Are we talking about the behavior stream and/or the "mind" in terms of categories that are defined, identified, and validated by the community of participants (emics) or by the community of observers (etics)? Four types of knowledge stem from these distinctions:

Emics of Thought
Emics of Behavior
Etics of Thought
Etics of Behavior

Each of these types of knowledge is allowable as scientific knowledge in conformity with the criteria set forth in step 1. In providing scientific knowledge about the emics of thought and behavior, the observers employ public, replicable eliciting operations (questions and answers) aimed at discovering how native participants view behavior streams and mental events, using categories that are deemed appropriate by the participants. While scientific knowledge of the etics of thought may also involve eliciting operations (as in psychological testing), the categories are imposed by the observer and need not be deemed appropriate by the native participants (as is also the case with etic behavioral descriptions).

3. *Bio-psychological givens.* The theoretical principles of C.M. depend upon the existence of certain empirically warranted biological and psychological needs, drives, and functions as universal attributes of *H. sapiens sapiens*: sex, hunger, thirst, sleep, nutrition, metabolism, digestion, vulnerability to mental and physical disease and to stress by darkness, cold, heat, etc. This list remains open-ended and responsive to new discoveries about the human biogram and population-specific genetic differences.

The epistemological significance of these innate human qualities is that they provide the basis for developing "currencies" for measuring the inputs and outputs of sociocultural systems, thereby making it possible to measure optimizing behavior.

Currencies amenable to costing under C.M. include energetic efficiency, nutritional costs and benefits, morbidity and mortality rates, power and wealth differentials, allocation of sexual privileges, etc. Conspicuously absent from this set are currencies directly linked to reproductive success and inclusive fitness. These mainstays of sociobiology do not enjoy the status of empirically established drives, needs, or functions in *H. sapiens sapiens.* There is no physiological or psychological evidence that reproductive success *per se* is capable of reinforcing responses; nor is there any evidence that cultural response repertories co-vary with genetic instructions established through differential reproductive success. High reproductive success and inclusive fitness (large numbers of direct and collateral offspring) may contribute under certain circumstances to the optimization of biogram needs and drives, but so may low reproductive success under other circumstances. (Farmers with large families may be optimizing health and well-being, but so may white collar workers who have small families.)

Naturally, behavior which confers no reproductive fitness on anyone will lead to group extinction; but the issue is whether *differential* reproductive fitness co-varies with the selective retention of cultural innovations.

4. *Infrastructure:* The components of social life which most directly mediate and facilitate the satisfaction of biogram drives, needs, and functions constitute the causal center of sociocultural systems. The burden of this mediation is borne by the conjunction of demographic, technological, economic, and ecological processes found in every sociocultural system. More precisely, it is the etic behavioral aspect of the demo-techno-econo-environmental conjunction that is salient and hence it would be more precise (but too cumbersome) to designate the causal center as the "etic behavioral infrastructure." Infrastructure constitutes the interface between nature in the form of unalterable physical, chemical, and biological constraints and culture which is *H. sapiens sapiens'* primary and variable means of optimizing health and well-being. It is the unalterability of the laws of physics, chemistry, and biology therefore that gives infrastructure its strategic priority in the formulation of cultural materialist theories. Cultural optimizations must in the first and last instance conform to restraints of nature.

5. *Structure and Superstructure:* In addition to infrastructure, every human sociocultural system consists of two other broad categories of phenomena: structure and superstructure, each with its mental/behavioral and emic/etic aspects. Structure denotes the domestic and political systems, while superstructure denotes the realm of values, aesthetics, rules, beliefs, symbols, rituals, religions, philosophies, and other forms of knowledge including science itself.

6. *Basic Theoretical Principles of C.M.:* The basic theoretical principles of C.M. are as follows: a) Optimizations of the cost/benefits of satisfying biogram needs probabilistically determine (select for) changes in the etic behavioral

infrastructure; b) changes in the etic behavioral infrastructure probabilistically determine (select for) changes in the rest of the sociocultural system. The combination of a and b can be called the principle of infrastructural determinism.

It is essential to clarify the epistemological status of the principle of infrastructural determinism. This principle is not a theory (nor is C.M. a theory). It is a guide or set of instructions for the production of theories. Hence it cannot be falsified. But the theories which are produced under its auspices must conform to the criteria of scientific acceptance as set forth in step 1 above. Under what circumstances then would one abandon such a principle? Only if it can be shown that there are alternative principles which are more productive of better, scientifically acceptable theories.

Quitting Early

What are research strategies good for? Do we need them? The value of a research strategy lies in its ability to sustain a commitment to theoretical principles even in the face of events and puzzles which seem not to conform to or to actually contradict those principles. Without this commitment, the intellectual and practical effort needed to develop an integrated corpus of theories will never be made. Instead, researchers will "quit early" and declare that the refractory puzzle cannot be solved and that the principle itself must be abandoned.

The propensity to "quit early" in regard to infrastructural determinants is characteristic of the idealist and eclectic strategies that have dominated much of anthropological research. Idealists hold that causal priority must be sought in the realm of mental emics and superstructure and reject infrastructural determinism as a matter of principle. Hence, they can scarcely be expected to produce materialist explanations, least of all when confronted with refractory puzzles. Eclectics reject the advocacy of either idealism or materialism, accepting any principle of causality or its absence as equally plausible. This results in an especially cryptic form of "quitting early." Eclectics claim to approach sociocultural puzzles with open-minded and even-handed fairness, yet they are unlikely to persist long enough to demonstrate infrastructural causation in any but the most obvious and superficial cases.

Eclecticism and Quitting Early

Robert Lowie's treatment of food preferences and aversions illustrates the effects of eclecticism on theory building. Lowie professed a typical eclectic combination of belief in the "potency of economic forces," with the belief that it is possible to turn the tables on infrastructural determinism and to show that culture is ruled by irrational values. Despite his advocacy of a balanced even-handed approach, and despite his reputation for hard-nosed empiricism, Lowie repeatedly "quit early." As a consequence he became the most prolific collector of examples of what he called "capricious irrationality" in preferences and aversions involving domestic animals and their products. On surprisingly slight empirical evidence, he flaunted example after example of idealist causation of foodways:

> Throughout Melanesia the pig greatly affects social prestige without noticeably adding to mass subsistence. (Lowie 1942, 541)

> The Zulu and other Bantu tribes of South Africa use milk extensively but hardly ever slaughter their animals except on festive occasions. On the other hand we have the even more astonishing fact that Eastern Asiatics, such as the Chinese, Japanese, Koreans, and Indo-Chinese, have an inveterate aversion to the use of milk. (Lowie 1966 [orig. 1917], 82)

> In Burma and in its vicinity—the probable ancient center of chicken-raising—poultry are not primarily kept for utilitarian purposes, and the eggs are hardly, if ever, consumed. What the natives mainly want is to use the thigh bones of the cock for divination. . . . In Unyoro fowls and eggs are never eaten. . . . Herders keep fowls nonetheless for magico-religious purposes. . . . Elsewhere in the interlacustrine region poultry are kept solely for sacred uses. . . . The Bambala take good care of their pigeons . . . yet "they serve no utilitarian purpose". . . . It is most important to note that while swine appear as domesticated animals in prehistoric Egypt, not one practical purpose for keeping them has ever come to light. . . . The Australian kept his dog, the dingo, without training it to catch game or render any service whatsoever. . . . We expend thousands for breeding race horses but have never taken up the milking of mares. . . . There are African tribes that churn butter only to smear it as a cosmetic on their bodies. . . . The Lango . . . will milk neither sheep nor goats. . . . People from sheer acquisitiveness will accumulate vast herds that cannot be economically exploited. . . . The Pangwe keep sheep and goats not to eat them . . . but mainly for the pure pleasure of possession. (Lowie 1938, 303-307)

> A Shilluk keeps hundreds of cattle, yet slaughters them so rarely that he is obliged to maintain his hunting techniques for an adequate supply of meat. His small cows yield but little milk, his oxen normally serve no purpose at all. But these Negroes, who have failed to perfect their dairying industry and who eschew a beef diet, expend enormous effort on massaging the humps of their beasts and twisting their horns into grotesque shapes. (Lowie 1960, 242)

These extravagant claims invited materialist refutations which demonstrated some degree of material utility for the allegedly useless items. Ultimately, of course, the principles of C.M. require not merely that there be benefits rooted in infrastructure and political economy, but that these outweigh the costs. In order to advance to this more difficult and problematic assessment, however, there had to be a phase of research in which it was sufficient merely to show that the irrationalist claims were false as stated and that Lowie had quit early.

The Melanesian pig problem was one of the first to be scrutinized and reinterpreted (Vayda, Leeds, and Smith 1961). Mass ritual slaughters of pigs were seen as both a provider of animal fats and proteins and a systematic regulator of warfare and environmental depletions (Rappaport 1967). Criticism has been directed at the strength and effectiveness of the homeostatic functions attributed to the peace-slaughter warfare cycle (McArthur 1977), but no one would wish to return to Lowie's view that pigs are raised in Melanesia "without noticeably adding to mass subsistence." As Morren (1977) points out, through intergroup rivalries and exchange, the Maring ritual cycle promotes increased meat production in a region conspicuously deficient in animal protein (Hornabrook 1977, 55). While there is waste, not everyone bears its burden equally, giving rise to political power based on the leverage of pig distributions and exchanges.

Another focus of reinterpretation was the East African cattle complex (Schneider 1957; Deshler 1965). It was established that (contra Lowie): 1) The restriction of beef eating to ritual occasions did not necessarily mean that meat would be available in larger quantities without the ritual restrictions; 2) concentration on milk rather than meat or blood might be energetically advantageous; 3) maintenance of large numbers of poorly fed animals can be a form of "banking" against drought and other disasters. As for Lowie's total loss dingo: 1) dingoes are sometimes (not never) used in hunt; 2) more often, semi-feral packs are followed and deprived of their prey; 3) the symbiosis between dingo and hunter is enhanced by keeping them as pets and letting them loose to breed; 4) dingoes are eaten as emergency food (Meggitt 1965; Harris 1986).

Although Lowie had not mentioned the sacred cattle of India, the prohibition on the slaughter and consumption of beef among Hindus is a classic example of an allegedly useless and harmful foodway which on closer scrutiny turned out to have many utilities and benefits (Harris 1966; Vaidyanathan et al. 1982; Harris 1986). Lowie's assertions about the costliness of the Chinese aversions to milk and the irrational aversion to mare's milk in the U.S.A. was also challenged (Harris 1968, 366-370). Lowie had no inkling that the digestibility of cow's milk is linked to population-genetic differences in lactase production among adults. Although the explanation of Chinese milk aversion involves more than lactose malabsorption (Harris 1977, 149 ff.; Harris 1986), past ignorance of this factor shows why premature "irrationalist" conclusions must be rejected.

Finally, Lowie's penchant for the bizzarre can be seen in his assertion that there was "not one practical purpose for keeping swine" in ancient Egypt. Swine were in fact eaten in dynastic times by followers of Seth, and their services were in demand for seeding and manuring crops (Darby, Ghalioungui, and Grevetti 1977, 171-199).

C.M. vs. Panglossian Functionalism

For proposing that changes in sociocultural systems are selected for in conformity with utilitarian principles, C.M. has been caricatured as a form of functionalism in which all is for the best in the best of all possible worlds (Diener et al. 1978). This accusation cannot be reconciled with C.M.'s longstanding focus on problems of class, caste, racial, and sexual inequality and exploitation (Harris 1959; 1964; 1971; Ross 1980; Murray 1980; Mencher 1980).

The fact that modes of production and reproduction are selected for in conformity with optimizing principles does not mean that every member of a society benefits equally. Where marked differences of power have evolved as between sexes and stratified groups, the benefits may be distributed in a completely lopsided and exploitative fashion. Under such circumstances the cost/benefits must be reckoned not only with respect to individuals in their infrastructural context but with respect to the political-economic decisions of power holders. Given ruling classes, no significant changes can take place which do not advance ruling class interests (except through revolutionary overthrow) but this does not mean, as dialectical materialists insist, that all changes which benefit ruling class interests necessarily have adverse effects on everyone else. For example, the rise of the service and information sectors in hyper-industrial capitalist societies reflects the higher rates of profit to be obtained from unorganized labor. An increasing portion of the hyper-industrial labor force consists of women who have to some extent risen above their previous condition as unpaid housewives and mothers dominated by blue collar male chauvinist husbands. There is no contradiction involved in holding that the greater advantages accruing to U.S. capitalist interests are facilitated by a lesser but still favorable balance of benefits over costs accruing to women. The behavior of both strata exhibits the predicted optimizations even though one might hold that the gain for women is slight by comparison.

C.M. is thus no less emphatic about the importance of political-economic inequality as a modifier of optimization process than are various dialectical materialists and Hegelian structuralists. Moreover full recognition is given to conflicts engendered by unequal allocations of costs and benefits between stratified groups and the system-changing potential of such conflicts. One can never escape the question of benefits for whom nor of costs for whom. Far from neglecting or covering up the effects of political factors on optimizations, C.M. recognizes regular systemic feedbacks from the structural to the infrastructural level which give rise to political economy, political demography, political technology, and political ecology. One cannot for example explain the adoption and spread of technological devices such as shotguns, high yield varieties of wheat and rice, tractors, or solar cell generators apart from the interests of trading companies, agri-business and petro-chemical transnational corporations, local landowners, banks, etc.

An example of political ecological feedback can be seen in Eric Ross's (1985) clarification of the optimizing behavior of the Irish peasantry during the great potato famine. Conventional wisdom has it that the Irish small holder adopted the potato simply because its caloric efficiency was greater than that of traditional cereals and because it could be grown on sandy, depleted soils. This supposedly had the peculiarly non-optimizing consequence of rapid population growth, the potato blight, catastrophic famines and the great mid-nineteenth-century migration from Ireland to the United States. Ross shows, however, that the behavior of the Irish small holder was as much a defense against exploitation as a preference for a new crop. English landlords forced the Irish peasantry out of subsistence grain production and onto marginal lands in order to make way for grain-fed beef for the English market. Potatoes were adopted as a last resort—the only crop that could grow on the land left for subsistence farming. Furthermore it is likely that the high rate of population growth was not a response to the potato but to the expansion of labor markets as is characteristic of less-developed countries today (cf. White 1982).

Feedback vs. Dialectical Unity

If the influence of conflict and of structural feedbacks loom so large as a modifier of infrastructural cost/benefits, what is the justification for separating infrastructural from structural components and according causal priority to infrastructure? The question is crucial because dialectical materialists take the position that since politico-economic considerations are decisive in class-structured societies, then political economy in the guise of the "social relations of production" should be considered part of infrastructure. C.M.'s rejoinder is that by lumping political economy with modes of production and reproduction, dialectical materialists sidestep the problem of explaining how the varieties of social relations of production were selected for. C.M. is an evolutionary paradigm in which the question of the origin of the state and its feudal, agro-managerial, capitalist, industrial-managerial, and hyper-industrial varieties is of paramount concern.

Much evidence from archaeology and history justifies the separation of infrastructure from the changing relations of production characteristic of the transition from bands to villages, villages to chiefdoms, and chiefdoms to ancient and modern varieties of states. Definite innovations involving the demo-techno-econo-environmental conjunction precede the emergence of new relations of production. The emergence of present-day forms of political economy is no exception. Hyper-industrial, military, trans-national corporations and bureaucracies rest on a foundation of high speed computers, aero-space rocketry, nuclear physics, instantaneous global communication via satellite, and rapid global transport of personnel and materials via jet aircraft. It is true that these technologies were products of military competition and the search for profits. As it is also true that the tendency to form conglomerates and trans-national oligopolies can be interpreted as contradictions inherent in the social relations of free enterprise capitalism. But this "inner dynamic" is subject no less than the inner dynamics of other sociocultural systems to the laws of physics, chemistry, and biology which place limits on the ability of of politics to control nature. Thus ultimately it is infrastructure that restrained and shaped what can be done in the name of optimizing military and economic interests among the superpowers and their clients.

Some of the differences between those who emphasize the effects of structure on infrastructure and those who emphasize the effects of infrastructure on structure can be reconciled if we bear in mind that the primacy of one or the other will appear to vary depending on the slice of time that is being observed. For example, if we break in on recent processes of change in China at a point just after the victory of Mao's revolutionary army, everything will seem to flow from structure to infrastructure and superstructure. Indeed, the communist ruling class was convinced that it could transform China by political exploitation and manipulation and rallied its forces with the slogan, "politics in command." The Red Guard movement and the Cultural Revolution were manifestations of this slogan. With the death of Mao, "politics in command" was revealed as fundamentally misguided and wasteful. The desired transformations could not be achieved on the basis of preindustrial technology, rampant population growth, and ideological rather than material rewards. In the light of the Chinese experience, it is difficult to understand how C.M.'s attempt to distinguish infrastructure from structure can be dismissed for lacking "pertinence to the findings of contemporary science" (Adams 1981, 603).

Superstructure

The most common and irritating misrepresentation of C.M. is that it either ignores the religious, symbolic, and other ideological features of sociocultural systems or regards them as mere epiphenomena. Since superstructural phenomena such as racial categories, food taboos, origins of universalistic religions, male sexist beliefs, revitalizations, witchcraft, voodoo, constitute some of the central puzzles of C.M., the charge of ignoring symbols and ideology can scarcely be sustained.

As for regarding superstructure as mere epiphenomenon or mechanical reflex of infrastructure, this is a figment of mechanical thinking among C.M.'s critics. In an attempt to discredit cultural materialist interpretation of India's sacred cattle complex, Freed and Freed (1981, 489), for example, assert that C.M. is aimed at contradicting the "common observation that religious beliefs can affect behavior." Yet the whole point of the original article in the cow debate (Harris 1966, 64) was that the taboo on the slaughter of cattle and the consumption of beef was not "useless" but "positive-functioned" (five such functions were listed). How can religion be an epiphenomenon if it is said to be responsible for "preventing the development of an agribusiness form of beef production for the elite and international market, slowing down the conversion to a landless peasantry, and lowering the rate of urban unemployment"? Indeed, the interpretation given by C.M. to the role of religion in sociocultural evolution is explicitly aimed at disassociating C.M.'s position from Marx's most famous remark on the subject:

> It is ironic, therefore, that Marx should have characterized religion as the "opium of the people." Under conditions appropriate for the development of messianic leadership, religion again and again has proved itself capable of organizing downtrodden and exploited masses into revolutionary armies. (Harris 1985, 457–458)

The key phrase here is "under conditions appropriate," that is, when infrastructure and structure render the mobilization of messianic revolutionary forces a practical possibility. This is what one means by feedback between infrastructure and superstructure. Superstructure affects structure and infrastructure, but it does so in conformity with the limitations and opportunities imposed on it by infrastructure. Thus superstructure can be system-maintaining or system-destroying depending on the balance of optimizations and conflicting interests in the rest of the system.

As in the case of political economy, the priority of infrastructure rests on the understanding of sociocultural evolution as a process. Understandings of the causal linkages in this process can be confused if one's observations happen to focus on the slice of time during which the superstructural feedbacks are in a system-destroying mode. At certain points in time religion is indeed an opiate; at other junctures, however, it can be a revolutionary and creative force capable of energizing masses of people for audacious assaults on citadels of power. But C.M., unlike eclectic and idealist strategies, denies (probabilistically) that the conditions for their mobilization can be created at the superstructural level. Nor is the ultimate fate of the movement determined at that level. For example, if we come in on the recent processes of change in Iran, we seem to be in the presence of a wholesale refutation of the principle of infrastructural determinism. One might claim that "Religion is in command," since it is the Islamic revitalization that toppled the Shah and humiliated the world's most powerful superpower by holding its citizens hostage for hundreds of days. But the systemic sources of these events are not to be found in the return to Iran of Ayatollah Khomeini from his exile in France, but rather in the despotic and exploitative colonial infrastructure which had been imposed on Iran in the aftermath of World War II. Similarly, the future of Iran's Islamic Republic will not be settled by the fundamentalism of the Mullahs, but by the secularizing trends of industrialization.

In positing an active, creative, but only temporarily dominant role for structure and superstructure, C.M.'s view of the causal processes of history are to some extent convergent with the position taken by French neo-Marxist anthropologists who have been influenced by Althusser and Balibar (1968). There is some truth in J. Pratti's (1981, 618) comment: "Harris and Godelier (when they are not being mutually antagonistic) are talking in different ways about 'determination in the last instance.'" However, C.M. holds that infrastructure is determinant in the first as well as the last instance. The strategic consequence of accepting Althusser's formulation (which arose out of the French Communist Party's attempt to explain how Stalinism came to dominate Soviet life [Thompson 1978]) is that the analysis of infrastructure gets delayed indefinitely while undivided attention is paid to the determinations of the structural and superstructural components. Having made the holy sign of determination is the last instance, the French structural Marxists proceed to act not like dialectical or historical materialists but like unabashed Hegelians or eclectics in the tradition of Robert Lowie.

Some of C.M.'s critics seek to discredit the division of sociocultural systems into infrastructure, structure, and superstructure as a nineteenth century atavism. While sharper and more operational sectionings of sociocultural systems may be needed and would be welcome, it will forever prove impossible to give scientific explanations of the evolution of cultural differences and similarities without identifying cross-culturally valid universal components of social life.

Contrary to assertions by some structural Marxists and other anthropologists who advocate a so-called dialectical approach, failure to distinguish etic behavioral components which maintain their form and function cross-culturally (Godelier 1977) can only lead to theories of small scope and little parsimony. Nor is it clear why anything is to be gained by collapsing the subsystems of the universal pattern into one indivisible whole. When this is done in the name of dialectics, dialectical strategies merge with eclecticism. But in the final analysis, as in all taxonomic endeavors, the value of C.M.'s etic behavioral infrastructure rests on C.M.'s ability to generate scientifically acceptable theories more efficaciously than rival strategies which operate with different categories.

One final excursion—or is it an alarum? While insisting that determinate causal processes operate in human history, and that human will and consciousness are dominated by infrastructural conditions, C.M. claims to be compatible with conscious attempts by individuals to control their own destinies and build a progressive sociocultural order. The opening for this volitional ingredient in C.M. is provided by the probabilistic nature of the determinism and the large degree of uncertainty that characterizes predictions in the behavioral and social sciences (cf. Magnarella 1982). If the influence of consciousness on history has thus far been negligible, it is not because of the immutability of the laws of culture and nature, but because of our failure to understand these laws and to consciously and intelligently optimize our welfare within the constraints they set upon us.

C.M., unlike dialectical materialism, does not provide a program for building a specific form of society nor propose a unity of epistemology, theory, and practice harnessed to a specific revolutionary outcome (e.g. the overthrow of capitalism). Yet C.M.'s epistemological and theoretical principles may in themselves be counted as a challenge to the status quo and as a contribution to progressive change in the sense that they call into question established wisdom concerning the relationship between ideas and behavior and thereby raise consciousness to new levels of awareness.

REFERENCES

Adams, Richard. 1981. Natural Selection, Energetics, and Cultural Materialism. *Current Anthropology* 22:603–624.

Althusser, L., and E. Balibar. 1968 (1970 translation) *Reading Capital.* London: N.L.B.

Darby, W., P. G. Ghalioungui, and L. Grevetti. 1977. *Food: The Gift of Osiris.* Vol. 1 New York: Academic Press.

Deshler, W. 1965. Native Cattle Keeping in Eastern Africa. In *Man, Culture, and Animals,* edited by A. Leeds and A. Vayda, 153–168. Washington, D.C.: The American Association for the Advancement of Science. Publication no. 78.

Diener, P., D. Nonini, and E. Robkin. 1978. The Dialectics of the Sacred Cow: Ecological Adaptation Versus Political Appropriation in the Origins of India's Sacred Cattle Complex. *Dialectical Anthropology* 3:221–241.

Freed, Stanley, and R. Freed. 1981. Sacred Cows and Water Buffalos in India: The Uses of Ethnography. *Current Anthropology* 20:221–242.

Godelier, Maurice. 1977. *Perspectives in Marxist Anthropology.* New York: Cambridge University Press.

Harris, Marvin. 1959. Labor Emigration Among the Mozambique Thonga: Cultural and Political Factors. *Africa* 29:50–66.

———. 1964. *Patterns of Race in America.* New York: Walker.

———. 1966. The Cultural Ecology of India's Sacred Cattle. *Current Anthropology* 7:51–66.

———. 1968. *The Rise of Anthropological Theory.* New York: Random House.

———. 1971. *Culture, Man, and Nature: An Introduction to General Anthropology.* New York: Thomas Y. Crowell.

———. 1974. *Patterns of Race in the Americas.* New York: W. W. Norton.

———. 1977. *Cannibals and Kings: The Origins of Cultures.* New York: Random House.

———. 1985. *Culture, People, Nature: An Introduction to General Anthropology.* 4th ed. New York: Harper & Row.

———. 1986. *Good to Eat: Riddles of Food and Culture.* New York: Simon and Schuster.

Hornabrook, Richard W. 1977. Human Ecology and Biomedical Research: A Critical Review of the International Biological Programme in New Guinea. In *Subsistence and Survival: Rural Ecology in the Pacific,* edited by R. Feachem and T. Bayliss-Smith, 11–20. London: Academic Press.

Kuhn, Thomas. 1970. *The Structure of Scientific Revolutions.* 2d ed. Chicago: University of Chicago Press.

———. 1977. Second Thoughts on Paradigms. In *The Structure of Scientific Theories,* 2d ed., edited by Frederick Suppe, 459–481. Urbana: University of Illinois Press.

Lakatos, I. 1970. Falsification and the Methodology of Scientific Research Programmes. In *Criticism and the Growth of Knowledge,* edited by I. Lakatos and A. Musgrave, 91–195. Cambridge: Cambridge University Press.

Lowie, Robert. 1966, original 1917. *Culture and Ethnology*, edited by S. Diamond. New York: Basic Books.

———. 1960. *Lowie's Selected Papers in Anthropology*, edited by Cora Dubois. Berkeley: University of California Press.

———. 1938. Subsistence. In *General Anthropology*, edited by Franz Boas, 282–326. New York: Heath.

———. 1942. The Transition of Civilizations in Primitive Society. *American Journal of Sociology* 47:527–543.

Magnarella, Paul. 1982. Cultural Materialism and the Problem of Probabilities. *American Anthropologist* 84: 138–145.

McArthur, Margaret. 1977. Nutritional Research in Melanesia: A Second Look at the Tsembaga. In *Subsistence and Survival: Rural Ecology in the Pacific*, edited by R. Feachem and T. Bayliss-Smith. London: Academic Press.

Meggit, M. J. 1965. The Association Between Australian Aborigines and Dingoes. In *Man, Culture, and Animals*, edited by A. Leeds and A. Vayda, 7–26. Washington, D.C.: The American Society for the Advancement of Science.

Mencher, Joan. 1980. On Being an Untouchable in India: A Materialist Perspective. In *Beyond the Myths of Culture*, edited by Eric Ross, 261–294. New York: Academic Press.

Morren, George. 1977. From Hunting to Herding: Pigs and the Control of Energy in Montane New Guinea. In *Subsistence and Survival: Rural Ecology in the Pacific*, edited by R. Feachem and I. Bayliss-Smith, 274–313. London: Academic Press.

Murray, Gerald. 1980. Population Pressure, Land Tenure, and Voodoo: The Economic of Haitian Peasant Ritual. In *Beyond the Myths of Culture.* edited by Eric Ross, 295–321. New York: Academic Press.

Popper, Karl. 1965. *Conjecture and Refutations: The Growth of Scientific Knowledge.* New York: Basic Books.

Pratti, J. 1981. Comments on Richard Adams's Natural Selection, Energetics, and Cultural Materialism. *Current Anthropology* 22:618.

Rappaport, Roy. 1967. *Pigs for Ancestors.* New Haven: Yale University Press.

Ross, Eric. 1985. Potatoes, Population, and the Irish Famine. In *Culture and Reproduction: Reconstructing the Demographic Paradigm*, edited by W. Hanwerker, 81–104. New York: Academic Press.

———. 1980. Introduction. In *Beyond the Myths of Culture*, edited by Eric Ross, xix–xxix. New York: Academic Press.

Schneider, H. K. 1957. The Subsistence Role of Cattle Among the Pakot and in East Africa. *American Anthropologist* 59: 278–301.

Thompson, E. P. 1978. *The Poverty of Theory*. London: Merlin.

Vaidyanathan, A., K. N. Nair, and M. Harris. 1982. Bovine Sex and Species Ratios in India. *Current Anthropology* 23: 365–383.

Vayda, A., A. Leeds, and P. Smith. 1961. The Place of Pigs in Melanesian Subsistence. In *Proceedings of the 1961 Annual Spring Meetings of the American Ethnological Society*, 69–77. Seattle: University of Washington Press.

White, Benjamin. 1982. Child Labor and Population Growth in Rural Asia. *Development and Change* 13:587–610.

Cycles of Violence: The Anthropology of War and Peace

ERIC R. WOLF

Some years ago, a playwright with anthropological proclivities, Robert Ardrey, wrote a book called *The Territorial Imperative* (1966). In this work he projected for us an image of Homo Sapiens, Man, as a killer-ape, thirsty for blood and hungry for meat, and ever bent upon murdering his fellow humans in defense of his home turf, his "territory." The implication was that man was innately aggressive, that murderous instincts were imprinted in his nature, and that he was destined therefore to make love incidentally, but war forever. But the evidence of Man the carniverous Killer is not all that clear-cut. Early African Pliocene-Pleistocene sites show us that early man did indeed kill some small animals, as do our closest primate relatives, the chimpanzees; but there is also a good deal of evidence to indicate that the mainstay of early hominids was not steak, but seeds, nuts, and possibly leafy plants. Whether or not and how frequently these early foragers killed each other is a moot point. Interpreting fossil finds by drawing analogies with the behavior of primates like baboons or chimps or that of social carnivores like lions or wolves have produced conflicting results. Variations in animal behavior —even variations among members of the same species or of closely related species—go hand in hand with variations in climate and topography, the presence or absence of competing populations, the nature and distribution of food resources, dietary preferences or commitments, physical capabilities, sexual dimorphism, social patterns of tracking and foraging, and the distributive consequence of sociability. No one rudimentary drive or instinct can account for such complex phenomena and their equally complex interlinkages. Palaeo-anthropologists have appropriately stressed the need to develop more carefully thought-out models that relate behavioral data more systematically to variations in bodily form and habitat (e.g. Boaz 1979; Peters 1979).

There are good reasons why analogies drawn from the behavior of primates or carnivores—or even more from unrelated species like stickleback fish and greyleg geese—can be applied to the study of human behavior only with the greatest of caution. Human beings do share their biology with other organisms; but biology does not only set limits; it also offers a range of capacities and potentialities. In human beings, aggression—like food-intake and sexuality—is processed through the operations of a large and complex orchestra of organs, the human brain. This brain furnishes the mechanisms through which we subject our drives to cortical control and monitoring; but the messages which release, direct, or inhibit behavior are not biologically implanted, they are learned. They are learned culturally in the course of human interaction and communication.

What is learned collectively and how such collective learning is played out varies widely among the peoples of the world. All human drives are subject to cultural transformations that put them at the service of quite different social, economic, political, and ideological arrangements. These arrangements dictate when and how we may fight, eat, sleep, and have sex. They also impose their own specific tensions and frustrations and offer characteristic channels for the release of such tensions and frustrations. The understanding of aggression in humans as opposed to greyleg geese—the wish and drive to injure someone and the ability to do so—must address itself to the specific character of the human condition, and thus to the human ability to generate widely different programs for the harnessing and transformation of biological energy in humans (see Holloway 1968).

Such programs, carried within the circuits of collective social communication, free us—"displace" us—from the animal need to respond to each situation in its separate terms. They set up rules on who to treat as friend, ally, or foe; when to fight, how to fight, how to stop fighting, what to do with the fruits of victory or the bitterness of defeat. Since they are not inborn, wired into our organisms, they are also capable of modification and change. The friends of yesterday may become the enemies of tomorrow; the enemies of yesteryear your future bosom pals. Love and hate may be re-directed; means and goals of conflict may be altered; swords may be beaten into plowshares. In the ability to generate such flexible programs lies another human paradox: the program may have false or imaginary premises and involve us in disaster; but it can also be corrected or replaced. There are, however, no guarantees.

To move closer to an understanding of war and peace, it will help if we first of all distinguish violence between people, interpersonal violence, from violence mobilized to fuel conflicts between entire groups. Interpersonal violence may be triggered by the wish to interfere with the activities of another person or to avenge some real or imagined wrong. It may result in killing, but it is not war. War proper involves entire social groups organized as political communities, and—intentionally or unintentionally—its outcomes affect the balance of power between such social groups and communities. Thus there are people who exhibit a minimum of interpersonal violence among themselves, but are bloodthirsty and relentless in carrying war to outsiders. The Mundurucú Indians of the Tapajoz River in the Amazon Basin studies by Robert Murphy (1957; 1960) are a case in point. There was very little conflict within a Mundurucú village, but massed collective violence against external enemies. Conversely, there are people who do not carry on war in the sense I have defined it above, who do not use massed violence to affect the balance of power among groups, but who nevertheless exhibit a good deal of interpersonal violence.

An exemplary case investigated by an anthropologist are the 470 Kung San or Bushmen of the Dobe region in the Kalahari Desert studies by Richard Lee (1984). The Dobe Kung acknowledge no overriding authority to keep people in line; they settle disputes through arguments, discussion, and through individual action in conflict. But just as they do not have an overriding state, so they do not make war. While Lee was in the field between 1963–69 there was little interpersonal violence, but his questions uncovered 81 cases of disputes: 10 major arguments without blows, 34 disputes involving fights without weapons, and 37 interpersonal conflicts with weapons. Arguments and fights without weapons involve both men and women; conflicts with weapons involve only men. Lee also turned up 22 cases of homicide by men and 15 woundings during the period 1920–1955, many of them occasioned by disputes over women. Homicides lead to other homicides; such feuds in fact involved 15 of the 22 killings (Lee 1984, 90: n. 2; 93–96).

It is thus clear that the Dobe Kung are not the "Harmless People" some have thought them to be: they fight and sometimes injure other individual Kung. They are familiar with individual violence but they do not carry on war; and this can be said of many hunting and gathering groups in the anthropological record. Julian Steward who studied the food-gathering Shoshoneans of the dry plateaus and mountain ranges of the Western United States wrote that

> In aboriginal times most of the Shoshonean people had no national or tribal warfare. There were no territorial rights to be defended, no military honors to be gained, and no means of organizing groups of individuals for

> concerted action. When war parties of neighboring peoples invaded their country, the Shoshoneans ran away more often than they fought. Hostilities generally consisted of feuds, not organized military action, and they resulted largely from the suspicion of witch-craft and from women stealing. They were therefore as often intratribal as intertribal. (1955, 112)

There were obligations to avenge the death of a relative, and these might be followed by reprisals and counter-reprisals. But "these were purely personal and could not involve definable suprafamilial groups, for such groups did not exist."

Mervyn Meggitt, who studied the foodgathering Walbiri —about 1,400 of whom live in small groups in the near desert-like environment of the Northern Territory of Australia—writes in a similar vein. When a man dies in a duel, his mother's brothers are charged with avenging his death either by seeking out the culprit who has fled to another community or by performing sorcery to kill him. This, Meggitt says, is as close as the Walbiri come to "the notion of intercommunity warfare" (1962, 245). Men want to fight as individuals; there are no professional warriors, no military leaders, no battle plans. He notes further that

> There was in any case little reason for all-out warfare between communities. Slavery was unknown; portable goods were few; and the territory seized in battle was virtually an embarrassment to the victors, whose spiritual ties were with other localities. (1962, 246)

Yet Meggitt also notes that in the past there was no love lost between the Walbiri and the Warramunga and Waringari to the west, and that men of both sides would combine hunting expeditions with raiding for women. These events would then set off counter-raids. At some point before the gold rush of 1909, too, the Walbiri drove the Waringari from native wells at Tanami and incorporated the area into their own territory. Meggitt says that by desert standards the engagement was "spectacular" and "uncommon" and that the participants in the raids thereafter met peacefully for ritual and trade at the Barinjanggu totemic site within Waringari country. But he also notes that in a country where wells are scarce and strategic resources, forcible seizure of wells may have been more common in the past (1962, 42).

What we learn from these examples is that among some human groups organized conflict between groups is absent or rare, and we can perhaps specify the conditions that account for the absence of war among them. All three populations—San, Shoshoneans, Walbiri—live in environments where strategic resources are widely scattered and seasonally variable. To survive, a person periodically needs to gain access to resources in other locations, and he gains such access through ties of kinship, marriage, friendship, and exchange. The Kung build these networks of friendship and neighborliness with people at different waterholes through marriage, visiting, the good will that comes with being someone's namesake or giving them gifts of ostrich-eggshell bead necklaces or arrows, spears, and knives. But there is no way in which a person can unilaterally live off the labor or resources accumulated by others. There are no surpluses to maintain a permanent leisure class, and no mechanisms other than those of kinship and friendship to gain access to other peoples' services.

Yet note that these conditions may not always have obtained in the past and may be subject to change, as environing circumstances change. The San may have been dominated in the past by Bantu-speaking pastoralists, and in the nineteenth century sold ivory, skins, and ostrich feathers to Bantu traders who supplied customers in Europe. It is thus possible that the San do not carry on war not because they live in the desert, but because they are marginals at the low end of a chain of unequal relations of exchange (see

Wilmsen 1983). Moreover, Lee notes that since 1948 the San have had increasing recourse to Tswana moots or courts to settle their disputes, that since 1950 increasing numbers have opted for wage-labor in the South African mines, that since 1980 many Kung increasingly have gone in for cattle-keeping, and above all—from 1978 on, Kung men have been recruited as trackers and combat troops into the South African army fighting the insurgent movement trying to establish an independent Namibia.

Similarly, the Shoshoneans were strongly affected by Spanish and American slavers who raided them for slaves (Bailey 1966). The case of one Shoshonean group, the Comanche, is noteworthy for a sudden reversal of their putative military passivity. When the Comanche received horses in the early decades of the eighteenth century this group, renowned for its previous avoidance of warfare, quickly became the scourge of the southern Plains and of the Mexican borderlands.

When we look at the Australian aborigines, we must also take note of the fact that the populations we see now are the survivors of a process of European colonization that first drove the aboriginal inhabitants from the more productive coastal areas and later appropriated much of the interior grassland to stock with sheep. The number of Australian aborigines is estimated to have declined from 300,000 to 40,000 by the beginning of this century (Reece 1974; Stevens 1972). We cannot know what environing conditions in military response may have been before colonization.

Two studies from the tropical and relatively well watered northern coast of Australia suggest that massed violence may have been more frequent there than in the desert. W. Lloyd Warner studied the 3,000 or so Murngin people of northeastern Arnhem Land in 1926–29. He noted that in addition to the usual individual or small-team raids to avenge a death or adultery, there were two *gaingar* or "regional fights involving a large number of clans" during the twenty years preceding his stay. These had involved 15 and 14 deaths respectively. In all, he estimated the total number of killings during this twenty-year period at 200 and argued that such removal of young men from the pool of marriage partners multiplied the marriage chances for the survivors and thus constituted a major factor in Murngin polygyny (1958, 158, 173).

Hart and Pilling, discussing the 1,000 or so Tiwi of Melville and Bathurst Islands, noted that disputes, fights, and duels were common; the overwhelming number of them were concerned with seduction and adultery. In 1928 a cumulation of cases of seduction and nondelivery on promises of bestowing daughters in marriage sent about 30 fighting men from the Tiklauila band into armed conflict with about 60 Mandiimbula. Yet, the authors note, military action remained individual and took place among disputes and arguments; "warfare, in the sense of pitched battles between groups aligned through territorial loyalties, did not occur and could not occur among the Tiwi" (1961, 83). The battle ended with the elders of both bands turning on a young trouble-maker and clubbing him unconscious. Among the Tiwi, women's work furnished an abundance of resources, and polygyny underwrote the successful collection and processing of produce. There was consequently much competition for women between elders and unmarried men, with corresponding tensions and conflicts. Hart and Pilling suggest that the unbalanced marriage ratio was due to extensive slave raiding and removal of young men by the Portuguese between 1600 and 1800, and subsequent "blackbirding" or capture in the nineteenth century (1961, 99).

This discussion should tell us that we should not extrapolate directly from examples of arrangements among hunters and gatherers of the present day to reconstruct what life and war might have been like among the first hunters and gatherers of human prehistory. Neither San, nor Shoshoneans, nor Australian aborigines are examples of pristine human kind; they have all been involved in the processes of European expansion and affected by them. What we can do is note the possible correspondence of resource scarcity and scatter and a tendency to expand interpersonal ties to reduce risks and increase survival chances. Under such circumstances there may well exist a motivation to limit violence, since it is unwise to make enemies of potential friends and allies.

At the same time, social life in such simple societies is frequently suffused with disputes over women. We must remember that we are dealing with small-scale groups that are often characterized as being "egalitarian," where there are no marked differences among men in their ability to occupy the culturally approved statuses and to reap the rewards that go with them. Yet precisely because a man needs a woman in order to become a fully fledged and recognized adult male, equal to other males, there exists a potential for conflict and inter-personal violence. Thus Jane Collier and Michelle Rosaldo have suggested that violence between men over women may be particularly strong in simple societies where men can become autonomous adults only when they can earn the rights to marry particular women by doing services for their potential fathers-in-law. There male autonomy depends on laying claims to women in competition with other men, and—once established—on being able to defend these claims against other men: "it is as husbands that individuals acquire the independence that makes them equal to other adult men" (1981, 295). Thus the striving for equality among men breeds displays of aggression.

> Because equality is the highest status available to men and because such equality is symbolically achieved through willingness and ability to use force, contests in which both sides demonstrate their capacities for violence provide the most appropriate means for affirming the equality that allows men to make peace. (1981, 294)

Needless to say such competition among men also makes for a good deal of autonomy for women, whose own politics of sex may exacerbate or reduce the occasion for conflict and hence for violence. Yet because these interpersonal ties of kinship and marriage, friendship and gift exchange, are ties between persons, there is also no reliable categorical and abstract mechanism that can mobilize human labor to the production and accumulation of surpluses. What can be multiplied are ties in people, not in land, pastoral range, or industrial resources. Thus there is no obvious translation of interpersonal aggression and violence into the acquisition of power over resources through military expansion and conquest.

Just such a tendency, however, makes its appearance when people apply labor to transform a piece of ground into a cultivated field or garden and with the acquisition of self-reproducing animals for stock. The greater the living manpower and womanpower of a social unit investing labor in field and range, and the greater the stored-up dead labor invested in these bases of subsistence, the more secure the unit, the greater the resources under its command, the greater also its capacity to engage in activities that yield prestige and influence. Where hunters and gatherers like the San or Aborigines disperse population, horticulturists and pastoralists aggregate them. They will do so by multiplying their families and adding new members through marriage. At the same time as long as they are not governed by an overarching authority, they must rely crucially on armed self-help. Populations that depend importantly on fishing grounds, hunting range, cultivated fields, or grazing lands thus face a double problem: to aggregate men to work, but also to aggregate men to defend crucial resources. And once you can aggregate men to defend land or range, you can also employ them to make others yield up land, range, or water.

The ability to aggregate fighting men for group warfare rather than for individual aggressive encounters is aided in kinship-ordered societies by patterns of social recruitment through marriage (Ember and Ember 1971; Otterbein 1968). Patrilocal marriage, where men separate their wives from their families of origin and bring them to live in the homes of their fathers and brothers, can serve to keep together a related group of males who work and fight together and may easily engage as a unit in disputes with other groups of men. In such groups the team of fighters is in effect an extension of the domestic organization of the household and of households related in the male line; and it can function as a cohesive interest group in maximizing the interests of the household cluster.

Such a situation is well illustrated in Mervyn Meggitt's work among the Mae Enga of Highland New Guinea (1965, 1977). Mae Enga are sometimes eager to attract outsiders to aid in clearing and cultivating lineage lands, either to add allies in case of war or to assist big men who are building reputations of wealth and prestige. At the same time, they understand that such recruitment of outsiders can produce conflicts in the future when the outsiders begin to press claims to retain land they have worked against claims of lineage mates for additional land; and the result may be bitter internal fights to expel the immigrants. On the other hand, Mae Enga will go to war against other lineages to incorporate their lands into their own. Meggitt's informants claimed that 58 percent of cases of intergroup conflict were over land, and in 74 percent of cases the victors seized all or some of the land of the vanquished. Mae Enga themselves understand war as an outcome of population pressing upon land resources.

At this point, however, we must also introduce a note of caution. The ratio of people to the food supply available to them may well be an important consideration in questions of war and peace. The Mae Enga view of these matters is subscribed to by many anthropologists as well as by proponents of military conquest to enlarge the *Lebensraum* of the conquerors at the expense of the conquered. Precisely for this reason, however, we also need to emphasize that population pressure does not always lead to military escalation on the Enga model. Among the Chimbu who occupy an area of the New Guinea highlands to the southeast of the Enga there is also violence and that violence often concerns disputes over land. But the Chimbu build stronger linkages than do the Enga between small segments of descent groups through marriages and ties on the maternal side. They lack the patrilineal ideology of the Enga that can mobilize many sub-groups into clan armies for concerted aggression and seizure of land from enemy groups. Warfare therefore remains limited to fights between smaller sub-groups, and is often inhibited by the pressure and mediation of in-laws and matrilateral kin (Brookfield and Brown 1963; Brown 1978, 280-284; Kelly 1968). Two lessons arise from this contrast. One lesson is that social entities organized hierarchically through vertical bonds and endowed with an exclusive and unilateral ideology will be prone to mass group members for warfare simply by converting their organizational charters into an order of battle. Under such circumstances, crosscutting ties that could mediate or reduce conflict are apt to be weak. This, in turn, yields the second lesson, familiar to anthropologists. If crosscutting ties are not weak, then there may also be no escalation effect, and peacefare may stand a better chance than warfare.

At the same time, the Enga case raises another important consideration regarding the military consequences of population pressure. The pressure of population upon the land is not direct, but mediated through a complex interplay of social organization and culturally formed aspirations. In Highland New Guinea a descent group needs land to produce food not only for people, but also for pigs—pigs raised to acquire women in marriage (women who will bear future warriors and care for future pigs), pigs to underwrite ceremonial feasts that will compensate past allies and attract new ones, and pigs to pay compensation in the case of homicide. It is pigs that make Mac Enga life go round, and it is the cultural complex of Mae Enga pig-keeping that triggers war between rivals but also peace among allies. It is thus possible to envisage a transformation in the nature of warfare through a transformation in the social and cultural mechanisms that constitute the present adaptation of people to their environment. In this regard it is also important to remember that these mechanisms and adaptation are not given for all times. They are themselves the outcome of processes of agricultural intensification and crop changes in the past (Golson 1982) and they may thus be subject to change or modification in the future.

The patterns of warfare we have discussed so far take place betweeen roughly symmetrical partners, between individuals or between groups roughly matched in resources and demographic potential. Such violence is therefore also self-limiting. Individuals may fight, but others who live with them will strive to defuse or settle the dispute through intervention and mediation. Politically organized groups may engage in war, but the very arrangements of kinship and marriage that allow them to mass people for work parties and war parties also inhibit the scope of war. You may setttle kinsmen upon conquered ground, but the fruits of their labor drawn from that ground will be eaten up by obligations of kinship; they will not be free and available for storage and deployment to widen and aggrandize a superior power. Kinship is thus distributive and not accumulative; and warfare reaches its limits when the limits of distribution are reached. Temporary warfare will give way to temporary peace when these limits are encountered. It is as if under such circumstances every increment of violence beyond that limit will produce a decrease in socially utilizable returns. There will thus be a tendency to re-establish a balance of power after the showdown, to fend off further violence through exchanges of gifts and marriageable offspring. "We marry whom we fight" is an axiom frequently invoked to limit the scope of conflict.

When we turn to consider more complex political entities—entities that are no longer ordered by kinship and affinity, but by commands from a political center—we also confront a marked escalation in the possibility and scope of organized violence. Such political entities are typically divided into surplus-producers and surplus-takers, one part of the population producing surplus in the form of tribute to supply a group of political specialists. These groups of political specialists are chiefs and their staffs and supporters in simpler situations, elite ruling classes in more complex ones. The flow of tribute underwrites a division of tasks and labor between the population at large and the political specialists at the center. At the same time it also creates the structural possibility of assembling a pool of laborers and resources specifically designated to support, widen, and enhance the instrumentalities at the disposal of the ruling group. In such a situation it is evident that the more producers you control, the greater the surpluses at your disposal, and the stronger the drive to aggrandize your fund of people and resources for war and through war. In these cases, therefore, massed violence in order to injure another territorial political entity becomes an important strategy in the pursuit of power.

Keith Otterbein (1970) has shown in a cross-cultural study of 46 societies that the less autonomous local groups are and the higher the level of political centralization embracing them, the more advanced the degree of military sophistication. Political entities directed by a central group of chiefs and states governed from a political center are more likely to possess complex military establishments with a professional army and a hierarchy of military authority than are kin-ordered bands and tribes. In addition, such societies are likely to wage war in order to gain political control over other groups. Power thus grows directly out of the barrel of a gun or a massing of the spears. But note that this is not a simple matter that renders war inevitable. First, if war becomes a political instrument of a dominant elite, it may be employed strategically, used to advantage, but shelved when disadvantageous. Thus an element of centrally organized and calculated rationality enters the deployment of violence by one center against another; organized peace becomes a possibility alongside of organized war. Second, how organized and massed violence is to be depends in part on the social and cultural characteristics and the interests of the ruling elite that handles that instrumentality. Thirdly, these social and cultural characteristics of the elite are related systematically to the ways the social hierarchies of order and domination are organized within the supporting society. Whether one goes to war or maintains the peace is no longer simply a matter of how many spears or guns one has, but a matter of the support, organization, and loyalty one is able to muster among the population at large. And, in the fourth place, making war or declaring peace depends on the state of your neighbors, their ruling elites and their social support base for war. Chiefdoms and states always move in a wider field of social and cultural relationships; and the state of that field is crucially relevant to the making of war and peace. You will perhaps be surprised that I speak of war, often seen as irrational violence, as an instrument of strategy with a potential for rationality. Yet, in so doing, I am trying to draw attention to the one avenue of hope that may yet extricate us from our present dilemma of fighting wars on an electronic inter-planetary battlefield.

Let us briefly look at the characteristics of "tributary" states. This is important for an anthropological perspective on war and peace, because states—including European states—were of this general type until the modern period, and because European expansion into the rest of the world after the fifteenth century encountered and transformed such "tributary" states into other kinds of structures. Each of these tributary states typically had a power center, an organization that could tax and collect tribute, mass people for public work projects such as the construction of roads, dams, and irrigation canals, pyramids and civic centers. They inhibited challenges to disorder inside the society and pressed their claims beyond their borders. Yet the power of such tributary states was never absolute, even in highly despotic societies. To carry out their functions, such states employed specialists, unarmed administrators who rule by writ of law (which is a promise to exercise power) and armed men. Yet the exercise of power through such specialists was subject to diminishing returns both internally and externally. Internally, the costs of administration and coercion might be too high, and the state might be forced to delegate power downwards. This amounted to a kind of contract in which lower level powergroups and powerholders were given a license to employ and exploit power in exchange for loyalty and services to the center (see McLeod 1982). As this downward delegation was subject to continuous negotiation, including negotiations by armed force, polities disintegrated and reintegrated. Frequently, such conflicts over internal negotiations provided an impetus to military expansion in order to furnish controllable resources for contending parties.

The archaeologist Tom Patterson has recently presented a most insightful account (1984) of how the conflicts over rights to succession within the ruling Inca elite of the Central Andes in the century before the Spanish Conquest led to the incorporation through warfare of new territories through which contending claims could be satisfied. Similarly, the Aztec state in Central Mexico first gained ground as a rising military power among contending but greatly weakened political domains, then organized itself by projecting internal conflicts into aggressive war, and then widened its ability to co-opt and reward its elite adherents through expansion outside the Valley of Mexico (see Brumfiel 1983). Vital to such consolidation and further expansion was always outright seizure of certain strategic resources: obsidian mines, cotton lands, and cacao groves in the case of the Aztecs; cottonlands, maize-producing piedmont, and llama-supporting puna as a base for wool production in the high Andes in the case of the Inca.

Yet in the case of tributary states such expanding power always reached diminishing limits of return when the state came up against contenders able to resist their onslaught. Sometimes these successful enemies were of the same scale and potential as the expanding power. Thus the Aztecs never were able to conquer Tlaxcala to their east and the Tarascan kingdom to their west. At other times, the expanding state came up against ecological limits and different social organizations supported by such different ecologies. The irrigation-based horticulture of the Aztecs encountered ecological limits in the arid desert country to the north, where they could not get an administrative grip on the stateless desert-dwellers of the Gran Chichimeca. The Inca similarly could not defeat the more fluidly organized Araucanians in the Chilean woodlands south of the Bio-Bio River or the inhabitants of the tropical forest to the east. Such areas contained resources favored by the center, but they could not be seized by war. Here trade took the place of war, furnishing gold, coca, forest peltry, and medicines for the Inca, turquoise or precious feathers for the Aztecs.

Internal heterogeneity and external limitation, however, also meant that such tributary states, even the very strong ones, contained important lines of cleavage. The Spaniards conquered the Aztecs in Mexico City in part through a new military technology—cavalry, cannon, and naval craft on the lagoons—but even more through enlisting on their side native rulers and populations in search of liberation from Aztec rule or of vengeance for past defeats. Pizarro's defeat of the Inca owes as much to divisions among the Inca elite—the conflicts between the rival brothers Huascar and Atawalpa—and to native auxiliary troops, as to Spanish military superiority.

The same phenomenon was in evidence when relatively small English armies encountered much larger Moghul armies in India. The Moghul armies were led by *mansabdars*, administrative officials of the state, each one of whom hired his own officers, who in turn would bring into the organization hired troops of his own. William Irvine wrote about this military organization that each soldier only obeyed the man directly above him, "and followed his fortunes studying his interests rather than those of the army as a whole" (1903, 57-58). The Chinese army in the nineteenth century was huge–120,000 Manchu, Mongol, and Chinese bannermen, under direct orders from Peking and some 500,000 to 600,000 members of the essentially Chinese "Green" Standard Army or constabulary (Wittfogel 1957, 66). Yet as these proved insufficient to contain the many internal rebellions, the government relied more and more on regional and local militias recruited by military commissioners appointed from the top or by local gentry, militias that became the prototype of independent warlord armies when the Empire collapsed.

Against such large and composite armies, but "essentially aggregates of individual heroic warriors" (Ness and Stahl 1977, 13), the Europeans deployed new kinds of military instruments. These were in part technological: the cannon-carrying sailing ship on sea and movable field artillery conjoined with individual small arms (matchlock muskets before 1600, flintlocks after that). More importantly, however, they were organizational. In place of assault by human waves, the Europeans–the Dutch first and afterwards the others–developed small industrial armies marked by precision and division of tasks in performance. This involved standardization of weapons and drill in the precise sequences of loading and firing, in marching and countermarching. It also involved the creation of standardized military units, organized hierarchically within a standardized table of organization. Finally, heroes were replaced with technically trained military managers. Ness and Stahl call these armies bureaucratic armies and see "the history of warfare as a continuous replacement of heroes with bureaucrat-technicians" (1977, 27).

The Europeans managed to subdivide and standardize both equipment and tasks while yet retaining a grip on the resulting diversity through the development of effective coordinating organization. This technical-organizational ability seems unusual in cross-cultural perspective and surely demands further study. It was perhaps influenced by the growing subdivision and synchronization of tasks both in agriculture and in arsenals and navy yards. Whatever future research may turn up in this regard, however, it seems possible to suggest a quite early date for the rise of the so-called industrial-military complex, if by this we mean the intertwining of military preparedness and supplies and financial sponsorship of such activities by private firms and states. These linkages also included an extensive arms trade and the ability to supply arms to allies.

Equipped with the new capabilities European expansion created the modern world as we know it. Economically, there came into being an international circuit through which wealth can now move to any part of the world and be deployed there as capital to mobilize resources and manpower. To this world-wide movement of capital corresponds a world-wide division of labor in which the varied regions of the world become specialized in the production of particular resources, now made available world-wide as commodities sold on an expanding market. At the same time, European expansion initiated a world-wide movement of people as colonists and laborers. Politically, there corresponds to this creation of a world-wide economic orbit the creation of major power blocs that now intertwine and affect each other on a world-wide scale. Instead of the regional entanglements and quarrels of the tributary states of the past—sometimes waxing into regionally potent empires and then falling back into local dismemberment—European expansion has initiated political rivalry in a global political and military arena. This began in the fifteenth and sixteenth centuries with the confrontation of Portugal and Spain, continued in the late sixteenth and seventeenth centuries in the confrontation of Holland and England, was followed in the eighteenth and early nineteenth century by the competition of England and France. It has now reached a twentieth century climax in the opposition of the United States and the Soviet Union. Each of these confrontations was fought out not only in Europe, but also overseas, in ever widening circles of involvement.

We have graduated from local conflicts between local population clusters fighting each other within narrow geographical orbits to world wars and military entanglements within a world system. This world system is currently dominated by two super-powers, the United States and the Soviet Union, in a situation foreseen by the Spanish diplomat, the Count of Aranda, in the eighteenth century. But the field occupied by the two super-powers is rendered vastly more complex by conflicts occurring on many different levels. We inhabit a world of multi-tiered conflicts. I will argue in conclusion that seeing all world conflicts in terms of the super-powers alone severely misreads the situation.

In the first place, there is the level of the super-powers themselves, each a complex growth with many differentiated external dependencies and internal cleavages, and vulnerable in that very dependency and differentiation. The tendency on the part of the super-powers to think that they are stronger than they are in fact constitutes a special source of danger.

In the second place, there are the contending powers of yesteryear, relegated to secondary positions that are each fraught with the potential conflicts produced by their removal from world power as well as by their need to maintain internal cohesion in times of crisis.

In the third place, there is a multitude of new client states, in large part created by European expansion. Many of these states owe their existence and development to the European need to find native collaborators in the nineteenth century or to ensure the supply and flow of globally required strategic commodities. Many such states are what Archibald W. Singham has dubbed "commodity states," operated by elites that trade political support and material commodities in exchange for capital and armament from elsewhere (see Singham and Singham 1973). Such states are arenas of internal competition over who is to exercise control and to benefit by the flow of credit and arms. This competition has produced what are sometimes called "internal wars," internal conflicts that have greatly increased in number and significance since World War I. Since these new states were often established through force and violence used against native populations, some of these internal wars are in turn, fueled by movements of resentment and resistance. In addition, such states are frequently compounded out of quite diverse populations, brought together either by conquest or by labor migration or both, and the mix of internal competition and resistance is then conjugated by ethnic divergence and conflicts over access to resources. All of these interlacing oppositions and contentions are cross-cut and exacerbated still further by competition among all states on all levels for the support and loyalty not only of their own populations, but for that of each other's population segments. World wars and internal wars are thus further intensified by encounters that tend to assume the character of "international civil wars," in which local contenders seek external allies and often find them.

The greatest single threat seems to be that all these arrangements of power and order are predicated not upon stable and enduring foundations, but upon an economic base forever trembling and subject to major quakes. The social and cultural arrangements under which people must lead their lives are forever being altered, altering the fate of people with them. In this continuous economic shuffling and reshuffling capitalism and the flow of capital has a special role to play. If capitalism has a special relation to the development of political freedom as we know it, it also exercises an extraordinarily destabilizing power in its continuous search for higher profits and sustained capital accumulation. Capital forever abandons older sectors of the economy and relocates in new and more promising industries and areas. Thus, as the playwright Bert Brecht once said, it is capitalism that is radical, and not communism. For in its continuous and often unpredictable movements, it also continuously shakes up the foundations of human existence, and as a result also calls into question over and over the capacity of power groups to wield power and to maintain it.

We are witnessing a case in point in the battles in El Salvador. There, as Carlos Cabarrús, S.J. has shown in his masterful book on the origins of the Salvadorean revolution (1983), share-tenants were increasingly cleared off the land after the 1950s to make way for the large-scale production of cotton, sugar, industrial crops, and cattle-keeping. Yesterday's share-tenants either flooded the cities or were relegated to the ecological margins to eke out a living as rootless proletarians. Cabarrús has demonstrated how this situation produced both the rebellion and the enlistment of the uprooted into paramilitary private armies run by staff officers and officials of the government. I conclude from this line of reasoning that in this complex world in which many people are walking about among the powder kegs carelessly lighting their matches, we must realize that the enemy is all too often ourselves. This is a situation that should cause us to beware.

REFERENCES

Ardrey, Robert. 1966. *The Territorial Imperative.* New York: Antheneum.

Bailey, L. R. 1966. *Indian Slave Trade in the Southwest.* Los Angeles: Westernlore Press.

Boaz, Noel T. 1979. Hominid Evolution in Eastern Africa during the Pliocene and Early Pleistocene. *Annual Review of Anthropology* 8:71–85.

Brookfield, H. C., and Paula Brown. 1963. *Struggle for Land.* Melbourne: Oxford University Press.

Brown, Paula. 1978. New Guinea: Ecology, Society, and Culture. *Annual Review of Anthropology* 7:263–291.

Brumfiel, Elizabeth M. 1983. Aztec State Making: Ecology, Structure, and the Origin of the State. *American Anthropologist* 85:261–284.

Cabarrús Pellecer, Carlos Rafael. 1983. *Génesis de una revolución: análisis del surgimiento de la organización campesina en el Salvador.* Centro de Investigaciones y Estudios Superiores en Antropologia Social, Ediciones de la Casa Chata, Mexico, D.F.

Collier, Jane F., and Michelle Z. Rosaldo. 1981. Politics and Gender in Simple Societies. In *Sexual Meanings,* edited by Sherry B. Ortner and Harriet Whitehead, 275–329. Cambridge: Cambridge University Press.

Ember, Melvin, and Carol R. Ember. 1971. The Conditions Favoring Matrilocal versus Patrilocal Residence. *American Anthropologist* 73:571–594.

Golson, Jack. 1982. The Ipomean Revolution Revisited: Society and the Sweet Potato in the Upper Wahgi Valley. In *Inequality in the New Guinea Highland Societies,* edited by Andrew Strathern, 109–136. Cambridge Papers in Social Anthropology no. 11. Cambridge: Cambridge University Press.

Hart, C. W. M., and Arnold R. Pilling. 1961. *The Tiwi of North Australia.* New York: Holt, Rinehart, and Winston.

Holloway Jr., Ralph L. 1968. Human Aggression: The Need for a Species-Specific Framework. In *War,* edited by Morton Fried, Marvin Harris, and Robert Murphy, 29–48. Garden City: Natural History Press.

Irvine, William. 1903. *The Army of the Moghuls, its Organization and Administration.* London: Luzac and Co.

Kelly, Raymond C. 1968. Demographic Pressure and Descent Group Structure in the New Guinea Highlands. *Oceania* 39:36–63.

Lee, Richard. 1984. *The Dobe !Kung.* New York: Holt Rinehart and Winston.

McLeod, Murdo J. 1982. The Primitive Nation State, Delegations of Functions, and Results: Some Examples from Early Colonial Central America. In *Essays in the Political, Economic, and Social History of Colonial Latin America,* edited by Karen Spalding, 53–68. Latin American Studies Program, Occasional Papers and Monographs, no. 3. Newark: University of Delaware.

Meggitt, Mervyn J. 1962. Desert People. Sydney: Angus and Robertson.

———. 1965. *The Lineage System of the Mae-Enga of New Guinea.* Edinburgh-London: Oliver and Boyd.

———. 1977. *Blood is Their Argument.* Palo Alto: Mayfield Publishing Co.

Murphy, Robert F. 1957. Intergroup Hostility and Social Cohesion. *American Anthropologist* 59:89–98.

———. 1960. *Headhunter's Heritage.* Berkeley: University of California Press.

Ness, Gayl D., and William Stahl. 1977. Western Imperialist Armies in Asia. *Comparative Studies in Society and History* 19:2–29.

Otterbein, Keith F. 1968. Internal War: A Cross-Cultural Study. *American Anthropologist* 73:277–289.

———. 1970. *The Evolution of War.* New Haven: HRAF Press.

Patterson, Thomas C. 1984. Exploitation and Class Formation in the Inca State. Unpublished MS. read at the annual meeting of the Canadian Ethnological Society, Montreal.

Peters, Charles R. 1979. Toward an Ecological Model of African Plio-Pleistocene Hominid Adaptations. *American Anthropologist* 81:261–278.

Reece, R. H. W. 1974. *Aborigines and Colonists.* Sydney: Sydney University Press.

Singham, Archibald W., and Nancy L. Singham. 1973. Cultural Domination and Political Subordination: Notes Towards a Theory of the Caribbean Political System. *Comparative Studies in Society and History* 15:258–288.

Stevens, R. S., ed. 1972. *Racism: The Australian Experience.* 2 vol. New York: Taplinger.

Steward, Julian H. 1955. *Theory of Culture Change.* Urbana: University of Illinois Press.

Warner, W. Lloyd. 1958. *A Black Civilization: A Social Study of an Australian Tribe,* rev. ed. New York: Harper and Brothers.

Wilmsen, Edwin N. 1983. The Ecology of Illusion: Anthropological Foraging in the Kalahari. *Reviews in Anthropology* 10:9–20.

Wittfogel, Karl A. 1957. *Oriental Despotism.* New Haven: Yale University Press.

Contributors

JOHN BENNETT is Distinguished Scholar in Residence at Washington University, St. Louis. His more notable works include *Of Time and the Enterprise*, *The Ecological Transition*, and *Paternalism in the Japanese Economy*.

ROBIN FOX is currently University Professor of Social Theory at Rutgers University. Included among his published works are *Kinship and Marriage*, *The Imperial Animal*, and *The Red Lamp of Incest*.

MARVIN HARRIS, Graduate Research Professor of Anthropology at the University of Florida, is best known for *The Rise of Anthropological Theory: A History of Theories of Culture*, *Cultural Materialism: The Struggle for a Science of Culture*, and more recently, *Good to Eat: Riddles of Food and Culture*.

VICTOR TURNER was the William R. Kenan, Jr., Professor of Anthropology and Religion at the University of Virginia. His works include *The Ritual Process*, *On the Edge of the Bush*, and *Dramas, Fields, and Metaphors*, as well as other well-known works in symbolic anthropology.

ERIC WOLF is Distinguished Professor of Anthropology, Herbert Lehman College and Graduate Center, City University of New York. Included among his publications are *Sons of the Shaking Earth, Peasant Wars of the Twentieth Century,* and *Europe and the People without History*.

KENNETH MOORE served as founding chairman of the Department of Anthropology at Notre Dame. His published works include *Those of the Street: The Catholic-Jews of Mallorca* and a new edition of *Revolt of the Masses* by José Ortega y Gasset.

Index